When it comes to keeping an orderly house, no one is hopeless—not even you! So, go and dig up a pencil (try looking behind the hutch—one rolled under there two years ago) and evaluate yourself by identifying your particular strengths and weaknesses. T or F:

____I am successful in using coupons.

____I still have my high school dance program.

____I plan my meals while I shop.

____I know how much I have in my checking account.

____I keep my bedroom door closed when I have guests.

There's more! For your score on this probing survey, see chapter 10.

If you're longing to welcome unexpected guests with open arms (instead of hiding behind a stack of newspapers)...if you're tired of fighting an avalanche every time you open a closet or cabinet door ... if there's a "Cleanie" inside of you who's striving to break free, then **The Messies Manual** will provide you with the humorous, helpful guidance and painless, practical tips you need to forever break away from chronic messiness!

THE MESSIES MANUAL

The Procrastinator's Guide To Good Housekeeping

Sandra Felton

Illustrated by Blanche Sims

Fleming H. Revell Company
Tarrytown, New York

Library of Congress Cataloging in Publication Data

Felton, Sandra.
    The messies manual.

    Bibliography: p.
    1. House cleaning.   I. Title.
TX324.F44   1984   648'.5'0207   83-16061
ISBN 0-8007-5133-7

To my mother, Seco Haley, whose example kept me striving for a better way of life when it was difficult to remember that another way of life existed.

Contents

I just love the story of Cinderella, don't you? One day Cinderella is living by an unpleasant fireplace dressed in tatters, getting dirty, working hard, never getting out for fun, and receiving no reward for all her effort. She was sad and frustrated. (Does it sound a little like your life?)

But the next day she is found by the prince, whisked off to the palace, and lives as a princess in a beautiful castle, never needing to turn her hand to clean house. And she lives happily ever after.

And who brings about this wonderful transformation? Why, it is her fairy godmother, of course!

For years I waited for my fairy godmother to come and wave her magic wand over me and magically change my hovel into a castle—and my frustration into joy.

But she never came.

There is magic to be found, but I was looking in the wrong place for it. The program you are about to begin will work its magic on you. You are about to enter the world of the Messie and the Cleanie. You will learn about the Mount Vernon Method, the Flipper System, and other secrets of housekeeping. Each chapter contains a little magic dust, and when you are finished you will be prepared to become that princess you dream of becoming.

But you must wave the wand. You must sprinkle the magic dust. And I know you will, because I know you won't settle for that stool in the cinders once you know that there is a castle waiting for you and that there is hope of finding it.

I want your home to be a castle, full of beauty and dignity. I want you to be a princess in your own home.

"Oh, no," you protest, "I'm not reading this book to get some kind of magic. I just want to be able to find my shoes, get the piles off the tables, and get my kids off to school with matching socks. I live a practical, mundane life. I just want to survive. I have no time or patience for fairy tales or dreams."

Maybe so. I know you would be satisfied if the house were just under control. This *is* a very practical book. You will be able to find that order you want.

But maybe, just maybe, after things begin to clear, somewhere in your house you'll find the corner of the castle.

God bless you, Princess.

Introducing

(AS IF YOU NEED IT!)

The Messie

We all know them. They are the people who never seem to get control of their housework and their time, the type who need all day to accomplish nothing. They live in dread of opening a closet door, for fear they will be buried under an avalanche of canned goods, flashlight batteries, tissue boxes, and stockings with only one run that might come in handy someday for something. (Well, you never know.)

A casual visitor to the home of such a person would be in constant danger of tripping over roller skates, knocking piles of paper to the floor, and stepping on a ten-year-old's pet frog.

But a casual visitor is not likely to get into this person's home. She won't even invite her best friend — not with the house in such a mess.

This type of housekeeper—if that is not too strong a term for a person whose house appears to keep her—has a name. She is known as a "Messie."

If you are reading this book, chances are you know her very well indeed, because she is you. Furthermore, you are tired of it. You are ready to take command of your house and your life—if only you can figure out how.

11

Perhaps, until now, you have felt yourself to be alone. You thought no other person could possibly have a house that looks as if a tornado has just struck it. And you have not wanted to talk about it, not wanted to do anything that might reveal your secret shame to the world.

Intelligence is the quickness in seeing things as they are.

GEORGE SANTAYANA

Well, take heart, because you are very far from being in a class by yourself. Millions of women—men, too—share your problem. And it's curable, or at least controllable.

I know. For many years I went through the same agonies you face, always searching for the answer to this terrible embarrassment. Finally, by studying my friends whose houses seemed always to be in order, I discovered some principles that I was able to apply to my own life and home.

The results were gratifying—so gratifying that I began to believe these principles might be of use to other struggling housekeepers. So I established the "Messies Anonymous" seminars to teach others what I had learned. To date, hundreds of housekeepers have attended these classes. Many have reported that what they learned has changed their lives for the better.

Literally dozens of these people have asked whether I would write a book that set forth the Messies Anonymous principles in greater detail. To help these people, as well as to reach others who may not be able to get to the seminars, I have written just such a book, and this is it.

May it be the beginning of a new, happier way of life for you.

The Procrastinator's Guide
To Good Housekeeping

Help!
House Out
Of
Control!

PART ONE

What's Your M.Q.*?
*(MESSIES QUOTIENT)

To cure anything—a disease, a stutter, an ingrown toenail—you first have to *classify* it. Try this short test:

YES NO

 Are all the spoons in your kitchen drawer neatly nested up to one another, while all the pots in the house sit in the sink and sulk? *See* The Perfectionist Messie.

 Did your mother have a "thing" about emptying bathroom wastebaskets? Is yours overflowing into the shower stall? *See* The Rebellious Messie.

 Would you love to come home and read the evening paper? Are there six papers currently residing by your favorite chair? *See* The Relaxed Messie.

 Are you still finding your teenager's baby teeth in the corners of the drawer in your bedside table?
See The Sentimental Messie.

 How long ago did you toss out your ironing board?
See The Spartan Messie.

After your dress comes back from the cleaner's, how long does it hang on the back of the kitchen door?
See The Clean Messie.

 Is it true that a gritty bathtub is less slippery than a sparkling one? *See* The Safe Messie.

Do you truly believe there is something sinful in serving children a pie from the supermarket?
See The Old-Fashioned Messie.

Have you figured out a simple solution to worldwide hunger, while your six-year-old learned to make toast in self-defense? *See* The Idealistic Messie.

1 | Messies Classified

A. The Perfectionist Messie

B. The Rebellious Messie

C. The Relaxed Messie

D. The Sentimental Messie

E. The Spartan Messie

F. The Clean Messie

G. The Safe Messie

H. The Old-Fashioned Messie

I. The Idealistic Messie

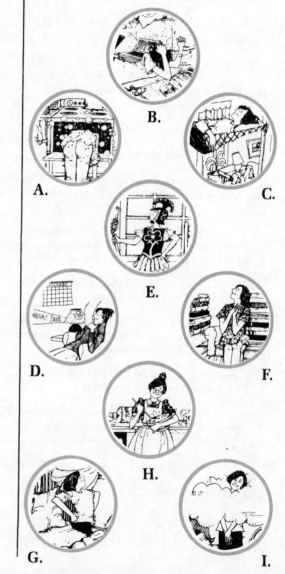

A.

B.

C.

D.

E.

F.

G.

H.

I.

M essies have one thing in common: On a scale of 0 to 10, on which 0 is disaster and 10 is perfection, their housekeeping falls into the 1–3 range.

This, of course, makes them the opposites of the housekeepers we know as "Cleanies," whose efforts are rewarded with a rating in the 7 – 10 range. It also sets them apart from average housekeepers — those whose homes fall into disarray on occasion, but not often and not for long, and who therefore merit a 4–6 rating.

Aside from their abysmally low housekeeping rating, Messies have little in common. They got to be where they are by different roads, and they have different styles of messiness.

Let us, therefore, take a look at different types of Messies. If you can recognize yourself in one of these word portraits, you will be well on the way to finding a solution to your problem.

The Perfectionist Messie

This person has very high standards for individual jobs. The house may be a wreck, but she decides to begin by cleaning the oven. And it is well done, *very* well done.

If you say, "No one sees the inside of the oven," she takes pride in saying, "But *I* know it is clean." In the meantime, the whole picture deteriorates.

Here, indecisiveness is cloaked in the guise of perfectionism. Generally this housekeeper cannot decide which approach to putting the house in order would be best. So she decides not to decide. This is a bad decision.

The Rebellious Messie

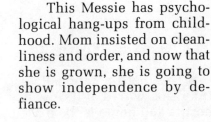

This Messie has psychological hang-ups from childhood. Mom insisted on cleanliness and order, and now that she is grown, she is going to show independence by defiance.

The tragedy, of course, is that we are adults now and it is a shame to let infantile reactions ruin our own lives and those of our families.

I heard a middle-aged woman say she had procrastinated for years about hanging a mirror even though it was in her way on the floor. The reason she didn't hang it was because the sight of the unhung mirror annoyed her mother, and she derived pleasure from the annoyance it caused. I guess she is showing Mom that Mom can't make her do it. But she is paying a high price for trying to show how grown-up she is.

19

The Relaxed Messie

This person rationalizes that the world outside is hostile and home is the place to relax. Why work at home, too?

So things are let go. The result is that when the rationalizer comes home from that high-pressure job, she faces a hostile house. Things assault the eye and clutter life.

How nice it would be to come home to a beautiful, inviting home that says, "Welcome," and invites us to relax! The truth, as any Messie can tell you, is that messiness is not relaxing. It causes strain, pressure, and jangled nerves.

The Sentimental Messie

Every scrap brought home by Johnny is precious. Every shell picked up on a beautiful day is valuable. We must keep our memories. I think memory is the source of the problem here. Some of us Messies have poor memories, so these things are the only way we can remember. When we throw them out, our memories actually *are* gone. In such cases, I suggest a memory journal. Write down the day's activities, especially the nice ones. These pages will be invaluable not only to you, but to your children and grandchildren.

Token remembrances also can be kept, of course, in easy-to-store, labeled plastic shoe boxes. But remember, keep only *token* items—not everything!

The sentimental Messie is also a picture-taking Messie. Pictures are another aid to a poor memory. Sometimes we don't even have to have them developed. We just like to know they are available for some time when we might get them developed.

So in virtually every drawer in the house, undeveloped film can be found. One woman said she had her film developed so late that she did not recognize the people standing with her in the picture.

The Spartan Messie

This is a special approach to the difficulties of house-keeping. The ancient Spartans lived with only the necessities of life. Similarly, it may occur to a Messie that if there were less to care for, or if it were somehow shut up or nailed down and not used, it would be possible to handle it.

The next step is to see what can be eliminated: "Let's see, I could always have one-pot dinners so I would have just one pot to wash. I could have one set of sheets so I'd just have to wash them and put them back on the bed, which would eliminate folding them or having them lie around in a basket. Or better still, I could make up the bed and sleep on top of the spread. That would eliminate washing sheets *and* bed making. I could clean up some of the other rooms and not use them anymore, just put a velvet rope across each door."

And so, to some degree or another, they cut out the things they have to handle. As a rule they don't actually get rid of them, they just exclude them from their care.

The Clean Messie

As long as things are clean, such Messies reason, they can be left out. This is the reason clean clothes are left in the basket and not folded. (After all, they *are* clean, and that's the main thing.) The dishes are washed and left out on the counter. But they *are* clean. Isn't that what counts?

The Safe Messie

This Messie leaves the bed unmade, "because it can air out better, and that kills more germs." The floors are not waxed, "because they might be slippery and dangerous." The dishes are not dried by hand, "because the germs from the dishcloth might get on the dishes. Air drying is more sanitary."

And finally, "I can't have a maid, because she might have a boyfriend who is a thief, and I'll be robbed." One cannot be too careful, after all.

The trouble with all these ways of thinking is that they tie us up and reduce our options for keeping the house the way we want it.

The Old-Fashioned Messie

For some reason, there are people who just enjoy doing things the old-fashioned way. For them, the only good way is the old way. This is a definite matter of principle—though it is hard to know what the reason is.

This might mean our Old-Fashioned Messie will have as a principle that the only way to do the floor is on her hands and knees with a brush. Now actually, the floor never gets done that way because it is too much work. But believe me, if it ever did get done, it would be done *right*. Their motto is "Do it right—or not at all." A lot of time it turns out "not at all."

Some other ideas the Old-Fashioned Messie may have are to bake pies and cakes from scratch instead of using a mix, to wax and buff the wooden floor with a cloth instead of a buffer, to beat the rug instead of vacuuming, or use cloth instead of disposable diapers. It's not that some of these things aren't appropriate sometimes, but to do things the hard way just because it is an old-fashioned way is a hindrance to progress in housekeeping.

The Idealistic Messie

This person's head is in the clouds. Great thoughts and ideas are what interest this Messie.

But the results are disastrous to an idealist. The beauty and charm, the satisfying family life, all melt under the heat of the messy home. The idealist, attuned to greater things, seldom notices the relationship between the messy house and the fading dreams.

In short, no matter what type of Messie you are, it's an unsatisfying life.

Confessions of a Reformed Messie

My mother was a Cleanie. What a marvelous thing it was in those days of my youth always to have a clean, beautiful house to come home to!

Keeping house seemed to come naturally to her. My drawers were always neat, my room in order. I functioned in the order she created. And she did try to train me, her only daughter. What a discouragement it must have been for her! I took to housekeeping like a cat to water.

We had spells when she did her best to get me in the groove and other spells when she gave up and found it was easier to do it herself. In the meantime, I had other things of greater consequence to do.

In high school there was school work. To me, studying was heady stuff. I worked on developing writing skills by turning out short stories and poetry. I took art lessons after school and was tutored privately in French.

Who in the world cared if there was dust on the table legs with art and philosophy hovering so excitingly close? Then came college, a career as

27

a junior high school math teacher, and marriage to a minister. Then I was on my own with a house to keep.

That's when I first noticed something seriously amiss. I found that the well-kept look, which had seemed to come effortlessly to my mother, didn't come to me at all.

At first I blamed the houses. The first one was too little. The next one was too big. I was sure there was just some small adjustment I needed to make in my situation and things would be all right. I was still busy with other, more important things. My husband was pastoring churches, and I was involved in his work. The children came, and I reacted to the housework. But I never controlled it.

Newton's second law of thermodynamics states that anything, left to itself, tends toward disorganization. This is especially true with houses. Felton's law is that "Any house left to keep itself tends to disaster." Murphy's law applied to housekeeping is, "Any mess that *can* happen, will."

It's tough being a Messie and a minister's wife. People like to drop around, especially if you are living in the parsonage right next door to the church.

Ivan's first church was in the northern Indiana farm region. Of Southern stock, I had grown up in Tennessee with its real or imagined tradition of frail womanhood.

These Indiana women were heartier than I was. They never even considered the concept of a "lady of leisure."

I once heard a parishioner talk about having done her spring cleaning. I was amazed that as part of it she had varnished the window sills with marine varnish. Most of our parishioners sewed, canned, had gardens, ran tractors, did church work, and kept neat homes, while I just wandered around trying to keep my head above water wondering what was wrong.

These women were gracious and never mentioned the gap between my abilities and theirs, which I felt so keenly. The worst part was that I could not figure out why they were succeeding and I was not.

In those days, as a young mother, I was able to tell myself that there was a *reason* for my poor housekeeping. More babies came, giving me further reasons. I was feeling better about my messiness now that I had collected so many good reasons. A really good excuse is a valuable thing. Several good excuses are a treasure.

The excuses satisfied my mind somewhat, but the soul is not so easily quieted. The frustration of not being able to find things, the embarrassment of having company drop in without warning, the hard work that never gets anywhere—there is no way to make these things somehow all right. They sap the joy from life.

It's really tough being a Messie.

excuse ik-'skyüs n. A perfectly reasonable explanation for the fact that your husband can't find the monthly bills ... or the checkbook ... or one pen that hasn't gone dry because someone left the top off for two weeks.

FELTON'S LAW: "Any Mess That Can Happen, *Will.*"

3

There Is a Reason— It Is Not Laziness

There is occasions and causes why and wherefore in all things.
WILLIAM SHAKESPEARE

Messies are generally wonderful people. Just between you and me, I think they are a cut above the average. They are creative, intelligent, nice people. My mother once answered a hundred calls making reservations for a class I was giving. She said it seemed to her that Messies were the nicest people in the world. One of the pleasures of having the class is meeting such interesting folks.

Messies are optimistic. Not many people could keep on going in the face of such discouragement and still hold on to such good humor. Fatigue and frustration take their toll at times, but somehow Messies keep going, looking for a better day.

If Messies are so wonderful, why, then, do they live "that way"? The reason is that housekeeping, though it seems to be a natural skill, is really a complex grouping of small, learned skills. If we are weak in one or several of these skills, we can run into all kinds of trouble in housecleaning and never know why. It is like someone who is color blind but not aware of it trying to make a career as an interior decorator: he or she would be gravely handicapped.

"Why are you late for dinner? I left you behind at the supermarket—again?"

"What petrified meatloaf in the oven?"

"Your briefcase? I put it in a safe place. Well, I must have *thought* the laundry hamper was safe!"

"What do you mean, you need a guide dog to navigate this room?"

"Socks? I'd have them sorted, but do you realize everyone in this family wears the same white socks?"

Most Messies are "handicapped" by several factors. One characteristic common to Messies is absentmindedness. We seem to have difficulty remembering the simplest things.

Poor Memory

I have a terrible memory, but it used to be worse! I frequently locked myself out of my car. Sometimes I would arrive at an appointment, only to discover that I had left an important piece of material behind. Worse, sometimes I forget the *appointment* itself! Once I left my purse with our entire life savings in it on a park bench. Another time I left my son at the junior high school where I teach math. I simply went home without him!

But if my memory was bad away from our house, it was equally so at home. It failed me so often that I used to be afraid to put anything in a drawer for fear I would forget where it was, or even that I had ever had it. Bills would pile up as I thought, *I'll get to them as soon as I can. I'll keep them out here so I won't forget.*

Then another item which I was afraid to put away would go on top of them, and then.... Soon there would be another "special" pile with who-knows-what in it beside the other piles of things too important to put away. The bill would be gone for good, or at least removed from the area of my influence.

Sometimes we Messies come to grips with some big cleaning project, organize the thing elaborately and well, and then forget what our organizational plan was. "Where *did* I plan to put these papers?"

"Out of sight, out of mind," is a statement of real truth where I am concerned. I cannot tell you how many times I have let the tub run over because I turned on the water, went off to do something else while it filled, and forgot the whole thing. Fortunately, we don't have wall-to-wall carpeting, wooden floors, or an apartment below us.

Forgetting where I am going, losing my keys, letting the bathtub overflow—are these patterns peculiar only to me? While absentmindedness is not limited to Messies, my guess is that it is more common among us. But why do we tend to be absentminded?

Distractibility

One reason for our absentmindedness may be that Messies tend to be easily distracted. If something grabs our attention, it is as difficult for us to ignore it as it is for a cat to ignore a mouse.

We notice a good book and begin reading it while cleaning the bookshelf. We take an item from the drawer or closet we are cleaning to put in a better storage place, but first we have to clear a place for it. Messes spring up like ant hills because of our big housecleaning project. Cleaning this way is tiring and messy, too.

If a person flits from one job to another—straightening this, clearing that—that's distractibility. Often a job is begun, the phone rings or a child interrupts, and the task is left, or worse, forgotten. An absentminded person usually cannot do two things at one time. Distractibility is akin to absentmindedness.

One of the stories I like best is of the absentminded professor who met a student as he crossed the campus. The two stopped to talk. When they finished conversing, the professor asked the student which way he had been heading. When the student told him he had been heading toward his office he replied, "Good, then I have eaten," and continued happily on his way. Now that's absentminded!

Disorganized Thinking

Another reason Messies tend to be absentminded is that clutter muddles our minds. A messy house stimulates further distractibility in us, which results in absentmindedness, which results in more clutter. It's a downward spiral. Consider the words of a Cleanie wife who lived with a Messie husband:

"I need order like an alcoholic needs a drink or a smoker needs a cigarette. I become irritable and disconsolate without it, unable to work or even to think straight. I am miserable."

But why are some people more organized than others? Some people are born organized, and some are not...or so it seems to me. It may be due to something in the nervous system.

Studies have been done relating right- or left-handedness to organizational ability. The theory is that people who are ambidextrous (who can use either the right or the left hand) tend to be disorganized because the brain gets signals from different sources and has difficulties in establishing organizational patterns. A person who is strongly right- or left-handed keeps using the same routes in the nervous system and therefore finds it easier to do the tasks that require organization.

After I graduated from college I did a survey on how people knew their right hands from their left. The typical reply was, "You just know." This was not too useful to me because I didn't "just know." If, therefore, you are not quick to tell one hand from another, you might be consoled—a little—to know that your inability to organize is not so much your fault as your nervous system's. It is good for batters in baseball and for sculptors to be ambidextrous—but it is bad for organizers.

Visual Tune-out

This has nothing to do with being unable to see. It does have to do with having what you see register. Some of us are not very quick on the visual uptake. When my family passes an accident scene, my husband and children see many more details than I do: "Did you notice the woman in the front seat of the blue car and the woman and little boy beside the station wagon?"

I am doing well if I notice the cars. Given enough time, I would pick out the details, but it doesn't come quickly or easily as we drive by.

Now apply this idea of visual sensitivity to housekeeping. Cleanies are visually alert. They want to see clear, clean, uncluttered lines. If they finish a cup of coffee and don't want another one, the cup is gone, swooped up to the kitchen and sometimes washed, rinsed, and put away in order to maintain the clean lines of orderliness. A Cleanie friend once told me she wished she *could* tune-out a fluff of thread on the carpet—but she *had* to pick it up, no matter how tired she was.

A Messie, on the other hand, can tolerate a great deal of clutter simply because she is not sensitive to visual things. An educator would say the difficulty is a lack of response to visual stimuli due to a figure-ground problem. No matter what others call it, when company comes to the door unexpectedly, we call it embarrassed.

Slow Movement

This usually isn't because of slow muscle movement. Some jobs take a long time to figure out.

Sorting laundry is the worst for me. There are five people in my family. After my eyes send a message to my brain telling me what they see, my brain has to figure out two things: whose piece of clothing it is and which of the piles in front of me belongs to each respective person.

Every piece of clothing requires this process. All that thinking can wear a person out, especially if the piles to be sorted become too large. I've discovered that I can save energy by sorting the laundry while the piles are small and manageable. I also put the piles in the order of the ages of family members. Then I don't have to figure where each pile is.

That speeds things up a lot. However, I have seen folks sort laundry zip, zip, zip — and they don't even seem to be thinking. The point is that if a person processes information slowly he is not going to be able to work as fast as others who do not have the same difficulty, and this can make house-keeping slow and fatiguing.

Sometimes, too, the idea of doing a job perfectly slows a person down. The job has to be *so* good that as a result, one little corner of the house is clean while the rest is still cluttered.

If you have one of these problems, or all of them, can you still hope to take charge of your house and your time? Yes, you can! I know, because I have done it.

To get some clues as to how this is possible, let's take a look at some Cleanies I have known and what we can learn from them.

4

Cleanies
I Have Known

These I have loved: white plates and cups, clean—gleaming.

RUPERT BROOKE

U nlike Messies, Cleanies have mental schedules they themselves are not aware of. Their minds are like computers going down their list of things to do.

The power that activates the computer is in the eyes. Again and again they say, "When I see..." or "If it looks dirty, I...."

Their goals are visual, and they become uncomfortable if something is out of place. Cleanies are not afraid to use shortcuts because they are confident in their own cleaning ability and don't feel it necessary to prove anything by doing things the hard way.

They tend to get up with a bang and get going with purpose. They frequently have a time goal in mind and work fast to meet it. You might think they are uptight people. They don't seem to be. In fact, they often are gracious, warm, and creative. They can afford to be because they have enough time to do whatever they want to do!

These are general statements, of course. Let's meet some of these paragons individually, to see if we can learn to do as they do.

One thing my Cleanie friends have in common is that they don't understand. They don't understand at all. I can always tell true Cleanies by the way they react when they hear that I teach a class on housekeeping. They look blank— very blank.

"Oh, it is a class on cooking."

"No, housekeeping."

"Oh, I see, a class on interior decorating."

"No, actually it's *housekeeping.*"

"Oh."

Silence. How can you continue discussing the inconceivable? Why would anybody need a class on housekeeping?

One blank-faced woman told me soberly that if I did have a class on housekeeping nobody would come. Since I had been having well-attended classes, I asked her why she thought nobody would come.

"Obviously if people have messy houses it is because they want them that way. And, if they want them that way, why would they attend the class? So nobody will come."

If Cleanies only knew how we struggle! But housekeeping comes so naturally to them that they don't understand at all.

It follows that the best way to learn from Cleanies is to meet some of them and watch them in action. And that is precisely what we are going to do now.

Carmen

Carmen works full-time in the import-export business. She is a widow and has a daughter eleven years old.

Going to her small condominium is refreshing. It is beige in color for warmth, but shining and cool to the touch. She has a floor of Italian tile and a lot of glass on tables and shelves. Vertical blinds regulate the light.

She herself radiates style. Most of her wardrobe is beige and black so that she can mix and match freely. Accent colors bring variety to her look.

Carmen has developed several tricks to keep her house beautiful without working at it. She freely admits that she dislikes housework and has better things to do. So she plans not to do it.

When her husband was alive he used to put the white pillows from the couch on the floor to watch TV. When she bought a new couch she bought one with attached pillows so that she would not even have to say anything to him about not putting the pillows on the floor.

Carmen also had a counter top that stuck out beyond the wall which divided the living room and kitchen. It fairly begged people to stick something on it as they passed. So they obliged.

Carmen didn't want to have to hassle people about this, so she had her husband extend the wall so the counter was not exposed and tempting. When she bought shelves for her living room, she bought the kind with glass in front so she would not have to dust as frequently.

Since Carmen's condominium is small, she does not have a dirty clothes hamper. Instead, she folds dirty clothes and puts them in a decorative chest at the foot of her bed.

Carmen uses "little minutes." She never cleans cabinets. When the cabinets are nearly empty, she wipes them out. When the refrigerator is nearly empty, she gives it a quick cleaning. When she puts her clean, folded laundry into the drawer, she gives the drawer a quick straightening. So there is no need for a cleaning marathon. She used to have a dog, but deliberately hasn't replaced it since it died. She is finished and ready to go at 9:00 or 9:30—A.M. that is!

Joyce

Joyce is a former 10. She used to pull her refrigerator out from the wall weekly and clean behind it. Now she is more relaxed and cruises at a comfortable 8 or 9. Joyce, an artist, is also a collector of trinkets. I do not recommend the trinkets. They are nothing but trouble when it comes to cleaning.

Joyce is married and has an eight-year-old boy, a long-haired dog, and two cats. She works at home full-time as a wife and mother.

If you ask Joyce whether she has a schedule she will say, "No," and then add, "but of course, I do the kitchen floor on Mondays. I don't have to, but I usually do. And I change sheets on Friday." And on and on it goes.

Joyce keeps a more casual schedule than Carmen and is finished about noon. When I say finished, I mean finished!

Then she is ready for painting. So she paints for a while, watches television, puts away the paints, cooks dinner, and welcomes her family home. It sounds so easy, doesn't it? But I remember days of full-time homemaking when I had the same amount of time and *never* finished.

How does she do it? The key can be found if we listen to what Joyce says: "When I *see* dog hairs, I go over the floor with a dust mop." "I put the paints away because I don't like to *see* them left out. It looks cluttered." "I think it *looks* nicer when the clothes are all put away." Cleanies are very visually oriented and want the house to look pleasant.

Joyce also uses little minutes shining the bathroom mirror with a dry bath towel each day after she brushes her teeth.

Marcella

Marcella had a lot of trouble telling what schedule she kept. One thing she did know, she was usually finished by 9:00 or 9:30 A.M.

Marcella is married, has two children, aged six years and five months, and baby-sits for a one-year-old. She also has a short-haired dog.

Her main principle is to keep her house in order so that she never has to do a big cleaning job. She gets up at 5:30 or 6:00 A.M. to feed the baby. She gets her six-year-old, Ginny, up at 7:00 A.M. to leave for school at 8:00.

Ginny is ready by 7:30 and plays with the baby until 8:00. Then the baby is ready for a nap, and Ginny is ready to go to school. From 7:30 to 9:00 or 9:30, Marcella does all of her cleaning.

At 7:30 she cleans the kitchen, does the dishes (no dishwasher), vacuums and mops the kitchen floor, and wipes the counter. Then she makes the two beds (five minutes), wipes down the bathroom (ten minutes), and does a few other chores.

Tuesday and Thursday are her free days when she is finished by 8:00 or 8:30. Monday and Friday are heavy days, on which Marcella works until 9:30, because they are at the beginning and end of the week. Wednesday is a moderate day when she does a little catching up for the middle of the week.

What does she do on the heavy days? She vacuums two bedrooms, one bath, and the den, then dusts the furniture and goes over it with window cleaner. Every day while she does the cleaning, she puts in two loads of laundry to wash, dry, and fold so that everything is done at the same time, and she doesn't have to worry about housecleaning for the rest of the day. She wants to be free for whatever comes up that day, whether it be business or pleasure.

How does she maintain the house during the day? She puts things away at once.

What does she do the rest of the day? She visits with friends who have children so the children can play together, goes to a painting class, and cares for personal needs such as nails and hair washing.

Of course, Cleanies' tricks of organization don't come naturally to us Messies — that's our problem. Nevertheless, with some thought, we can develop devices that will help us keep our homes as orderly as those of our Cleanie friends. (Well, nearly!)

First of all, though, let's take a look at some of the attitudes that get in our way.

Once upon a midnight
    dreary,
There I stood, my eyes all
    bleary.
'Mid coffee cup and Twinkie
    wrapper—
How I yearned to be a
    midnight napper!

But once upon a morning
    bright,
I'd vowed to clean before the
    night.
Though ambition fled before
    the noon,
I still refused to change my
    tune.

Once upon a dawn less
    dreary,
My whole house shone,
    spotless and cheery.
And though no one would
    know but I,
I claimed a victory with my
    sigh...

...and woke the kids for
    breakfast.

5 Outlooks That Hinder

The mind is the key to what we do. Sometimes we slip into a pattern of thinking that hinders us from making progress, and we never realize that while our wills are saying, Go, go, our minds are saying, No, no. So we end up failing because we are harboring pet ideas that keep us from going forward. We have to be willing to make some changes in the way we think if we are ever going to make permanent changes in our houses. In this chapter are attitudes that need to be dealt with if we are going to succeed. These may include some of the outlooks you, personally, will need to change.

Task-Orientation

People who say, "I've got all day to vacuum the rug," are indicating that they are going through the motions of housekeeping and doing the job just to get it done, not because it is an important part of a larger picture. As long as we look at housekeeping as a group of isolated tasks lined up in order to be done, we can put them off because there is no reason to do them except to get them off the list.

The solution is goal-orientation rather than task-orientation. We should never lose sight of our overall goal, which in this case is an orderly house. When we see our work in terms of this goal, individual tasks become a means to an end.

Let's look at it this way: Suppose two people are given two different jigsaw puzzles. The puzzles are identical except that one has a beautiful picture on it that cannot be seen or enjoyed until it is assembled, while the other one has no picture, only gray pieces. If you ask the first person what he is doing he will say, "I am making a beautiful picture." If you ask the second person he will say, "I am fitting together one piece after another. After a while I will have each piece fitted in." The first person is goal-oriented, the second is task-oriented.

A person who is task-oriented can wait all day to vacuum the rug, as long as it does get vacuumed that day. A person who is goal-oriented, however, won't wait all day since his goal is to maintain a nice-looking house at all times, and a dirty rug will short-circuit that goal.

Practicality

Why put the toothpaste away if you are going to get it out again in a few hours? Why make the bed just to unmake it that evening? Is it practical to wash a few dishes? Why not wait till you have a whole sink full and do them all at once? These ideas are practical, but they delay your reaching your goal—a beautiful house.

The Myth of Creative Disorganization

Everybody knows creative and intelligent people can be very disorganized. Some creative people are deliberately disorganized. Have you ever seen the sign on a desk that says, "A neat desk is a sign of a sick mind"? This is some disorganized creative person taking the offensive.

Frequently, however, this clutter interferes with the fullest use of the creative gift. Imagine the writer who can't find his paper or research material, or the artist who misplaces supplies. Looking for things saps the creative process.

Losing things is a sign of disorganization. A book called *The Borrowers* attempts to explain how items just "disappear." This book tells of little people who live under the floorboards and behind the baseboards of houses and "borrow" things. *That's* why they disappear.

A lot of these little people used to live at my house. However, they must not like living in organized houses, because since I organized mine they seem to have moved out.

Idea-Orientation

Messies are intelligent people on the whole. We have high ideals and a worldwide perspective.

World hunger, dedication to the children and youth of our nation, art, music, literature, careers — these are areas that deserve our time. Dusting, moving a dish from one place to another—how can such things be important in the light of such weighty pursuits? They seem insignificant by comparison.

The trouble is that if we are disorganized at home we can lose our chance to do something about the problems we consider more important. How can we finish our book if we can't find the first six chapters of it? How can we organize a drive to ease world hunger if we can't locate the addresses of the people and organizations we need to help us?

Psychological Hang-ups

Because Messies are born with a problem when it comes to organization, housekeeping has frequently been a problem from childhood. If Mother is a Cleanie, the situation can be frustrating for both Mother and child. Mother can't understand why the job she gives her child is so poorly done or only half-completed.

The child, on the other hand, may think she has done it well, or she may have been distracted by something else and forgotten that the job was not completed.

Mom becomes frustrated and sees this as evidence of an uncooperative spirit. The child may be surprised to learn that the job is poorly done; she cannot understand why Mom is so upset. She becomes resentful at what seems to her to be unjust criticism.

So housekeeping becomes associated with unpleasantness early in life. It is only a short step from here to the idea that housekeeping causes frustration and should be avoided. After all, if you don't try it, you can't fail.

Depression or Emotional Upset

One of my worst periods of housekeeping was at a time when I was going through a trying emotional experience in another part of my life. I felt as if I were walking in molasses; things just didn't get done. Whatever a person's weakness is, it gets worse during such times. My bad housekeeping became my terrible housekeeping.

I don't believe I would have been able to respond to help in organizing my house during that time, even if help had been given. I had to wait until the psychological problem righted itself before my housekeeping returned to merely "bad."

Frequently, however, the housekeeping actually causes the depression. The feeling of being out of control and the problems caused by poor housekeeping can lead to such despondency that housework is further neglected, and a destructive downward spiral begins.

Sometimes this is accelerated if some overwhelming event occurs. A flood, hurricane, earthquake, or some natural disaster which further messes up the house can easily destroy all hope of ever getting control.

A less traumatic event, such as your mother moving, with her furniture, into your already crowded house; the moving of furnishings from an office which has been closed into your place for storage because there is no other place to keep them; the starting of a home business requiring storage of some items—any of these may bring about the breaking point.

If housekeeping is causing you depression, the only way I know to overcome it is to start to reverse the downward spiral by taking control of things. It is not easy to begin; but one success, however small, will lead to another, and slowly a pattern of success will emerge. Remember, it took you a long time to get into this situation, and it will take a while to get out. The important thing is to be heading in the right direction. You are allowed to get discouraged occasionally, but not to give up.

Always remember, too—you don't have to aim for perfection. In fact, as you will see in the next chapter, a too perfect house can be as bad as one that is chaotic.

You Don't *Really* Want to Be a 10

Extremes are always bad. Once in a while you hear about people who have been found dead in their homes because some trash has fallen on them as they walked through the passageways left by their walls of junk. Such a person is a 0 on the Cleanie scale. No 0's would come to a Messies Anonymous seminar or read this book.

Once, when Messies Anonymous had just begun, we had a ½ come to the seminar. He had disposed of his kitchen appliances so he would have room for more items. He had shelves lining his walls and set up in the middle of his rooms, library style. They held all of his many collections.

He subscribed to thirty-eight magazines a month and kept them all, envisioning the value of a complete collection. He was now starting to store some things outside.

The reason he came to the seminar was to see if we knew of any way to store more things in his, by now, decidedly limited area. Coming to our seminar for this reason is like going to Weight Watchers to inquire if anybody knows where bigger clothing can be bought.

The odd thing was that I felt upset that evening, not because of John—he could live however he wanted—but because his story stirred up in me the desire to have thirty-eight magazine subscriptions and a room full of shelves. That is a scary and uncomfortable feeling. I know how much harm indiscriminate gathering can cause.

The feeling went away by the next day. I wonder if I would feel the same discomfort now that I have broken the gathering habit.

But if a 0 (or ½) is an extreme, so is a 10. When I was a child, we lived in Memphis, Tennessee, where it gets very cold in the winter. From time to time I would hear the children of a neighbor begging to come in out of the cold, but their mother wouldn't let them in. When I asked my mother why, she told me the neighbor didn't want her children messing up the house. When we went over to her house I was warned not to touch anything or move around much. This woman was an example of a 10.

We also lived next door to a woman who used to hose down her house after it rained because the rain had splattered dirt on the outside wall. I went into her house. It looked like a model home. I commented that she must have just had her kitchen cabinets painted. "About seven years ago," was her reply.

Don't ask me how she did it. Her husband spent a lot of time down the street in a bar and took his shoes off at the front door when he did come in. That's a 10 for you—hard to live with.

We don't want to be either a ½ or a 10. Those who rate from 4–6 are average housekeepers. Their houses are satisfactory most of the time, varying with the circumstances. A 4–6 would not be likely to come to a Messies Anonymous class unless she was dissatisfied with being average and wanted to be a more efficient housekeeper. Some have come and found the class helpful.

The 7–9 group are Cleanies. This is a generally wonderful group, and I admire its members a great deal. As I have already suggested, if we Messies want to get our own houses in order, Cleanies are the people we must emulate. But where do we begin?

HOUSEKEEPING LEVEL   TELL-TALE SIGN

- ☐ 0 No one cares to enter your house.
- ☐ 1 Fools rush in where angels fear to tread.
- ☐ 2 If you *had* to, you could find at least one clean towel.
- ☐ 3 The dishes are clean, but stay out of the upstairs bath!
- ☐ 4 At least once a week, everything's spotless— for a day.
- ☐ 5 You can read a book without overwhelming guilt.
- ☐ 6 The minister's wife can call without panicking you.
- ☐ 7 You can hold elaborate luncheons twice a week and have everything neat by 3:30 P.M.
- ☐ 8 You gave away the dog and made the kids understand.
- ☐ 9 Your children aren't allowed downstairs, except to eat (neatly).
- ☐ 10 No one dares to enter your home.

Turning
Things
Around

PART TWO

Goal-Setting: He Who Aims at Nothing Is Likely To Hit It

You got to have a dream,
If you don't have a dream,
How you gonna have a dream come true?
OSCAR HAMMERSTEIN (*SOUTH PACIFIC*)

If you don't know where you are going, there is no need to start. Perhaps those of us who had Cleanie mothers have one advantage over those who did not—we know how nice a clean house can be. How lovely it is to have one's drawers neat and tidy. How lovely it is to bring friends home and be proud of the decor and the order.

If your mother did not leave you this legacy, then you can pick it up now from friends whose homes you admire. In our church we have frequent get-togethers in homes of various members of the congregation. At first I thought they had just fixed things up for the church get-together, but when I went into the back bathroom or the garage, or chanced to look in an open closet door, and saw the same neatness there that I saw in the more public areas, I was sure this was the way they always lived.

Halloween was also a revelation. At that time, when mothers walked their little tots around trick-or-treating, I would move the clutter which was around the living room door out of sight and down the hall.

Then I would close the curtains that revealed the other parts of the house. From the vantage point of the front door, things were passable.

But I would see that my neighbors didn't have their homes curtained off. Their windows were open for viewing and, perhaps more startling to me, their homes were lovely. I didn't have time for beauty. I was just surviving. I began to dream that my house could be that way. I envied the well-placed figurine, the uncluttered space. It was a good envy. It made me want to change.

Daydreaming can be an excellent thing. Studies have shown that people who are high achievers are frequently daydreamers. They use daydreaming as a method of goal-setting. You can do that, too. Use creative daydreaming to work for you. My daydream is something like this:

I see clean, shining tabletops warmly reflecting the lamp and the well-chosen items on the tables. I see sunlight and leafy shadows playing across the vacuumed rug. I see my favorite colors artfully used, affirming that this is a place for me to be happy and comfortable.

I see my family moving happily in their home, clothes and food easily provided. I see myself full of energy because I am in control.

I see myself developing and growing stronger in spiritual ways, because I have time and energy for the Spirit. I thank the Lord for the opportunity to live up to my unique potential for my own pleasure and that of those around me.

Get out a piece of paper and write out your own day-dream. How do you want your house to look? Once you have written it down, you are on your way to achieving that goal.

It is valuable to state your goal specifically. When I set out to gain control of my house I had only a general, foggy idea that things had to be "better." But as I gave it further thought, I hit upon a goal statement that says it all: "I want my house to be like Marcella's."

You have already met Marcella, one of my Cleanie friends. I want my house to be like hers because hers is consistently neat, shining, and pretty. I was just there today, around ten in the morning. Marcella was caring for her six-year-old, home from kindergarten, her five-month-old baby, and a friend's year-old baby. What an invitation to chaos! But as usual, the house was spotless and even prettier than I remembered it. Obviously it isn't because she keeps people out; she is always willing to share her home with children and adults alike.

On the same piece of paper on which you wrote your creative daydream, write a sentence or two stating your goal. If you write it, your muscles will already be in the act and you will be starting to change. Set a five-year goal and a life goal, too.

Vaslav Nijinsky, one of the great ballet stars of all time, is legendary even today though he lived in a time when there were no moving pictures of his dancing. It is said that he could leap higher than any other dancer, five feet into the air, and hover there a second or two. Now, on the surface, this would seem to be an impossible task. When people asked him how he could do this, he replied, "It's easy! I just made up my mind to do it." He could not do it the day after he decided to, of course, but once a determined individual sets a goal, he finds a way to reach it. And he did.

In athletics, successful goal-setters abound. Tom Dempsey, who holds the record for kicking the longest field goal in NFL history, hobbled onto the field because he has only half a foot and wears special shoes. But he did the job. Boy, did he do the job! Obstacles are insignificant to a determined goal-setter. They do not disappear, they are just overcome.

I was watching the televised Olympics. A young American runner who had come in second was being interviewed. He told an interviewer that he would continue to train for four more years for the next Olympics when he hoped to win the first-place gold medal. "When you put yourself under the strain of training for four years for one race, what is likely to give out first? The legs?" "No," was the reply, "the mind."

"The secret of success," said Benjamin Disraeli, "is constancy to purpose." Winston Churchill said it another way: "Never give in, never give in, never, never, never, never—in nothing, great or small, large or petty—never give in except to convictions of honor and good sense."

The hardest part is keeping one's goal in view when the going gets rough and the end is not in sight.

That's why it is so important to write it down. If it is written, you have made a stronger commitment. If you have not written your goal yet, you can write it in the margin of this book. If you have written it on paper, store it in this book so you'll know where to locate it.

In order to reach this goal, you will need to welcome the three C's into your life. They are:

Change — There have got to be changes if things are going to improve. But change is hard to bring about. The way things are is at least familiar and somewhat comfortable, however unsatisfactory.

Perhaps the hardest changes to make are in the mind. The ideas that "creative people are messy," or that "a person with three preschool children cannot keep a neat house," or worst of all, "I am hopeless," must be changed or no improvement will come.

The truth is that we are all made in the image of God. God is not a God of disorder. This means two things. First, we are not happy living in disorder because it is against our natures. Second, we do have the power to control and order our lives.

When God first put Adam in the world, He told him to have dominion. We need to take that position in our homes— we are going to have dominion. I believe it is God's will that we take control of that portion of our lives which is our responsibilty and rule it competently and well.

Commitment — Commitment involves dedication to a project. If your house is really important, dedicate yourself to the task of cleaning it up. Put it at the top of your list of priorities.

Control — I have already told you what nice people Messies are. Some of us are too nice for our own good, and for the good of our families. We are the Room Mothers, the Cub Scout leaders, and the Sunday School teachers.

But we need to use good *judgment*. It is hard to suggest cutting back on such obviously worthwhile activities. Nevertheless, I am going to suggest that you do cut back. The good is enemy of the best.

Our first responsibility is our home, not for the sake of the house, but for the sake of ourselves and our families. The home is the base from which we reach out into the world. When our base is in order and we have a schedule of maintenance, then we can begin to add a little at a time until we see how much we can handle.

Here's where control takes over. If you have been known as a community worker, people will continue to ask you to do jobs. You must take control of your life. Make your decision in the light of your priorities and if necessary, say, "No, I'm sorry I won't be able to help you on that."

Sometimes you can suggest an alternative. If you are asked to bake cookies for a class party, ask if you can buy them. If requested to take part in a money-raising event, make a donation instead.

The hardest person to say no to is yourself. Your hobbies of ceramics, gardening, writing, painting, and friendships vie so pleasantly for control. If your top priority for right now is organizing the house, promise yourself and your friends that later, when things are different, you will return to your old acquaintances and activities refreshed and happy.

You have only a limited amount of time and energy. Spend it where it will help accomplish your goals.

THE DIAMOND OF SUCCESS

In housekeeping as in any other job we set out to do, there are factors that set the successful achiever apart from the frustrated wheel spinner.

What sets Cleanies apart from Messies? They have a formula for success whether they are consciously aware of it or not. This can be diagrammed by the diamond of success given below.

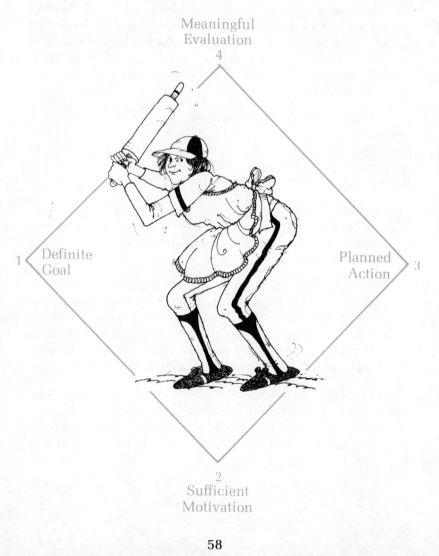

Meaningful
Evaluation
4

1 Definite
Goal

Planned
Action 3

2
Sufficient
Motivation

Let's apply them one at a time to our plan of house-keeping.

1. Goals—A goal must be specific in order to be meaningful or useful. Just to say, "I don't want to live this way anymore," is not enough.

How do you want to live? Make it clear by deciding something like this: "I see myself being able to have friends over anytime without three days work."

"I see myself waking up in the morning with the house under control and I see myself with a plan to keep it under control."

Emerson has said, "Thoughts rule the world."

Make your thoughts concrete. Even if you have done it before, write on this line your statement of your goal for yourself.

MY GOAL FOR MY HOUSE IS _____

_____

Remember: "He who aims at nothing will likely hit it."

2. Motivation—Athletes know that 90 percent of preparation is mental and 10 percent is physical. They know that many times they lose because they beat themselves, they psych themselves out. The main thing is to have a winning attitude. In order to win in athletics you must expect to win.

Use what is called the movie technique to get yourself going in the morning. See yourself doing the jobs you have planned, leaving the house with it in order, returning to a supportive house.

Now mix what you see with emotion while you are seeing it. Feel determined as you see yourself working, feel happy when you see your job completed.

3. Planned Action—Halfhearted doing will doom us to failure.

There is a verse in the Bible which says, "And whatever you do, do it heartily, as to the Lord," but you and I know that the big part of our problem is lack of knowing what to do and when to do it. That's why the Mount Vernon Method and the Flipper Method, described in Part Three, are so important. They give us a plan for getting the house organized and keeping it that way.

We can wear ourselves out just deciding what to do if we don't have a predetermined plan.

And once you decide what to do, do it heartily.

Remember the older woman who was asked for the secret of her lifelong success. She replied: "When I works, I works hard; and when I sits, I sits loose."

Work hard; **then** sit loose.

One word of warning. Don't plan to do so much in the beginning that you wear yourself out and quit. Pace yourself and take a day off each week.

4. Meaningful Evaluation—One temptation is to put a plan into motion and just keep on keeping on with it simply because it is our plan and not because it works. We need to stop and evaluate whether it works or not.

Mayor Koch of New York City is known for asking frequently, "How am I doing?" Stop and ask yourself, "How am I doing?"

Now that you have your goal set firmly in your mind, and have written it down as well, let's take a look at the five problem areas which often afflict the Messie housekeeper. Afterward, you will be given a test to help you determine which of these areas is causing you the most difficulty.

8

Five Pitfalls for the Wanderer in Messieland

As noted, problems with house-keeping seem to fall into five main categories. Some of them overlap a bit, but I am sure you can recognize them easily and pick out the ones that relate to you most strongly.

The usual problem areas are:

1. Storage or Organization. This includes maintaining orderly draw-ers and closets and the storage of seldom-used items such as Christmas things and light bulbs. Storage is the basis for what is to follow in other areas of cleaning. If you don't have a place for everything, how can you put it away?

Few people see whether or not we have messy closets, but they do see the results of it. If you have to look and look for the phone book, or keys, or whatever, this area needs work.

2. Neatness. Some people tell me they are disorganized in their closets and drawers but have neat-looking rooms. This is difficult for me to un-derstand since the same things that made me messy inside the closets, made me messy outside them, too.

A neatness problem is best identified by our feelings when people drop in on us unexpectedly. Much visiting has been done on the front porch because we aren't ready for unexpected callers. Many invitations have not been issued because it would take too much work to clean and organize. This is unfortunate because Messies are frequently warm, sociable people who would enjoy sharing their homes with others and entertaining friends. But the house won't allow it!

3. Paper. Where do all the papers come from? Children bring them home from school. Newsboys deliver them. The mailman brings his stack. Magazines come. We pick them up in stores. And occasionally people stick them under our windshields when we are at the store.

But we don't mind, do we? Papers have such fascinating stuff on them. Some of them have ideas, and Messies are very practical. Papers can also be very important. They can have to do with taxes, children's school activities, and so forth. We are especially infatuated with papers. And we love to keep them.

4. Bills and Banking. This is an area of life that requires organization or it falls apart. A bill makes no demands for a while, so it is easy to set aside and forget until it has gone into oblivion. Banking is the same way. The statement comes so quietly and so neatly packaged that the tendency is to let it stay closed up in its little envelope. At least that way the canceled checks will all be together in a pile somewhere. So long as they are there somewhere we are comfortable.

But that doesn't quite solve the checking problem. Some people attending my seminars have told me they keep two accounts and switch back and forth as the need arises in order to keep current with the balance in an account. One woman told me she has even changed banks, letting one account stand long enough to get it under control and to let all the checks come in. That was the only way she could know how much money she had in the account.

I understand this. For me the detail and tedium of the checking process is very difficult. Since I am distractible, I do not find it an automatic process to record every deduction and every withdrawal. Failure to do so, though, can cause havoc in a checking account.

5. Collecting. The word *collecting* is not the best word to describe this problem. *Collecting* indicates some order or design which in this case is lacking.

What I have in mind is the keen desire to gather lots of things because they "might come in handy someday." Or to keep them for the sake of the past.

Why do we love to collect so many things and have such a hard time throwing them out? Either we do it for the past or for the future. Certainly it isn't for the present, since the present is suffering because of all this stuff we are trying to live with.

We feel we have to hold on to things from the past because we are trying to preserve some beautiful memory. The things we keep are attached in our minds to some important person or event in our lives, and we keep them out of respect. This is a particular problem when the person whose things we are keeping has died. One of my seminar students felt compelled to keep several houses full of furniture because they were from the estates of deceased loved ones. The same woman had four closets full of clothes four sizes too big from her admired, deceased mother-in-law, whose memory she wished to preserve. A widow I knew felt that if she threw away anything that had belonged to her husband she would be throwing away part of him. My guess is that anyone who loved us would be the first to urge us to live our lives in the present and not try to hang on to the past.

We also try to keep things for the future—just in case we ever need them. We save for possible needs or emergencies that might come. Don't sacrifice the present for the future. That's no healthier than living in the past.

We also keep things because they are valuable. Everything has some value, no matter how small. I had occasion to take metal bones out of several bras. Do you know that I was reluctant to throw them away? *There must be something they would be good for,* I thought. *Maybe I ought to save them. Perhaps I could glue them together to make Christmas ornaments.*

It's true, there *might* be some use for them, but no one has appointed me keeper of everything which might have some value. That is too big a burden to bear — "keeper for the world." I threw them away happily when I realized I didn't have to think that way anymore.

My mother who, as you already know, is a Cleanie, told me yesterday of her latest garage sale. "It's so nice in the house now. I got rid of all the things I didn't use. Now the closet floors are empty and only what I need is in the drawers. It's wonderful, wonderful, wonderful!" From staying with her on visits I can tell you that living that way *is* wonderful. There is freedom in having no more than you need, no more than you can control.

But the collecting impulse is hard to control because on the surface it seems so logical. Why *not* keep that yarn? Someday you may learn to knit, and it will be wonderful to have your own supply already! (*If* you can find it.) Why not keep all prescription medicines? Someday your child may be very ill in the middle of the night and the doctor may say that only one medicine will help him. You'll look in the cabinet and find that you have that very medicine, even if it is ten years old. The doctor will say that it is better to have ten-year-old medicine than none at all, and you will give it to your child and he will be saved. So, you see, it is dangerous to throw anything away.

The problem with this thinking is that it just doesn't work. We gather and gather and gather good things, and some things that are not so good. Soon the pile gets out of control, and we can't find what we want when we need it.

Things control us and our lives. We begin to make adjustments in our way of life to accommodate all the "stuff" we have. We tell ourselves that we *can't* throw anything out. We end up with so much that it *is* a monumental task to clean or organize.

I am not saying that everything must go. But the collecting mania has to be taken in hand and controlled if we are ever going to get off the un-merry merry-go-round.

Not everyone wants to break the collecting cycle, but there's a good chance you do. You bought this book because you want to change and because you know there is more to life than amassing great globs of junk. You can avoid all of the pitfalls and problems that are part of the habit of hoarding.

One way to start is to identify which of the five pitfalls is your greatest problem. In the following chapter you can evaluate just exactly where you are in the vicious cycle of messiedom.

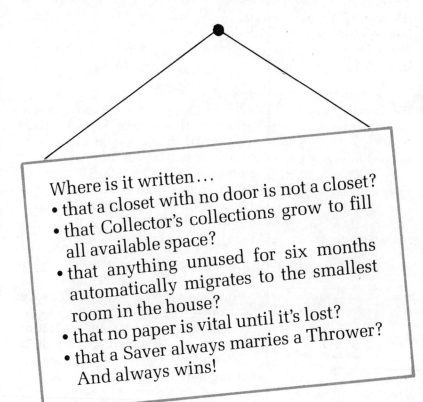

Where is it written...
• that a closet with no door is not a closet?
• that Collector's collections grow to fill all available space?
• that anything unused for six months automatically migrates to the smallest room in the house?
• that no paper is vital until it's lost?
• that a Saver always marries a Thrower? And always wins!

9 | A Personal Evaluation

N ow that you know the five major pitfalls that cause Messies their greatest difficulties, you will want to know which is your most significant problem area. The following evaluation exercise will help you get a handle on your strengths as well as your weaknesses.

Respond to each statement with the answer that best reflects your situation today. Resist the temptation to give what you think is the "proper" reply. Then, using the answer key, interpret your evaluation so you can see which of these problems needs the most attention in overcoming your "Messie" status.

Answer each of the following "true" or "false."

____ 1. It is hard for me to throw away newspapers because I might have missed something good in them.

____ 2. I am successful in using coupons.

____ 3. I have to work all day to have dinner guests that night.

____ 4. I follow a plan for bill paying and have a place to keep the receipts.

____ 5. I still have my high school dance program (or the equivalent) somewhere in the house.

____ 6. I have medicine over five years old in my medicine cabinet.

____ 7. I know how much I have in my checking account.

____ 8. I keep my bedroom door closed when I have guests.

____ 9. Having houseguests is next to impossible.

____ 10. I know what I would do with an extra shoelace or light bulb.

____ 11. I keep magazine issues that have good articles in them.

____ 12. I clip newspaper articles, but don't have any special plan for keeping and finding them.

____ 13. My trading stamps are under control.

____ 14. My matching sheets and pillowcases are together.

____ 15. My least favorite thing is for unexpected visitors to drop in.

____ 16. I decide what to have for meals as I shop.

____ 17. My cleaning materials are close to where I use them.

____ 18. Cleaning the stove is part of my regular cleaning.

____ 19. There are pieces of jewelry I can't find.

____ 20. I buy things I don't need just in case I might need them someday.

Answers

1. F *(C)*	6. F *(C)*	11. F *(C)*	16. F *(O)*
2. T *(P)*	7. T *(B)*	12. F *(P)*	17. T *(O)*
3. F *(N)*	8. F *(N)*	13. T *(P)*	18. T *(O)*
4. T *(B)*	9. F *(N)*	14. T *(O)*	19. F *(O)*
5. F *(C)*	10. F *(O)*	15. F *(N)*	20. F *(C)*

Evaluations

C = Collecting, P = Paper, O = Organization, B = Banking, and N = Neatness. Count up the number missed for each letter.

Multiply each C missed by 4.	My score is _____.
Multiply each P missed by 6.	My score is _____.
Multiply each O missed by 3.	My score is _____.
Multiply each B missed by 10.	My score is _____.
Multiply each N missed by 5.	My score is _____.

The problem area in which you made the highest score is likely to be the one you most need to work on. Still, this is not always the case. You may feel some other area causes you more difficulty. In that case, go with your own intuition about the matter.

Now list your problem areas from the biggest to the smallest. As you go about implementing your new housekeeping system, you will be aware of which areas require the most concentration on your part.

BIGGEST PROBLEM   1 _____

                                 2 _____

                                 3 _____

                                 4 _____

SMALLEST PROBLEM   5 _____

Once you have isolated your specific problem areas, it will be easier for you to take command of them. Now you are ready to get started on the road to good housekeeping. In the next section of this book I am going to share with you exactly how I took command of my house, the system that helped me get organized, and the tools that help me stay in control.

THE
SYSTEM

10

The Mount Vernon Method: How I Took Command

The first thing you need to know about in order to organize your home is the Mount Vernon Method. Some years ago during my desperate search for help, a Cleanie friend told me about the Mount Vernon Method. While touring George Washington's estate, my friend had been so impressed with the maintenance that she made a point of asking the woman who was in charge of housekeeping about the method they used.

The housekeeper explained that she directs her cleaners to start at the front door and work their way around the outside periphery of the room. When one room is finished, they proceed to the next, doing everything that needs to be done in each room so the rooms are left clean and organized. They dust and wax from the time they come to work early in the day until it is time for the public to arrive. A few minutes before opening time the workers collect their boxes of cleaning supplies and leave. Each day they begin where they left off the day before and keep going from room to room until it is quitting time.

But it is easy to clean Mount Vernon. George is not there to mess

71

it up! I decided not to use the method for dusting and polishing, for cleaning walls, drapes, upholstery, or carpets. First I needed to get organized. I started at the front door.

The first item of furniture beside my front door was a lamp table with one small drawer. After I had cleaned that little drawer, throwing away several very old school calendars, old classified ads, and a lot of junk, I felt I could do anything.

Next, I came to a piece of living room furniture that had six drawers, two of which literally had not been opened for years. I was actually afraid to open them. Why afraid? I think I believed I would not be able to handle what I found—that my decision-making apparatus would be sprung and broken.

But after a good night's rest, I did open the drawers. The challenge turned out to be a paper tiger. I could easily handle the things I found there. There were no terrible decisions to make. I am still surprised at the unreasonable fear I felt about those drawers.

As I continued around the house I threw out twelve-year-old medicine from my medicine cabinet. In my clothes closet I came across my wedding shoes. They were twenty-three years old, were missing a decorative buckle, and had never fit. However, I thought perhaps someday I might locate the buckle and they might come back in style. (You never can tell, you know. Miracles *do* happen!)

I threw them out. I wasn't going to let the past with its lovely memories muddle today. Messies are hopelessly sentimental.

You have to think about your total house organization. We think because we are capable in other ways we can handle anything. Yet even the most capable person can't work when things are disorganized. So think organization.

The most important thing about the Mount Vernon Method is that you pace yourself and not overdo. The temptation is to work like a crazy woman because of the frustration you feel. Don't start out too fast. You will not be able to accomplish the Method in a single day (it took me three and a half months to "Mount Vernonize" my home).

Think of this as a marathon as opposed to a sprint. Since a sprint is a short-term race, you start out giving it all you've got. For a marathon, however, you have to conserve at the beginning of the race because you know you have the end to think about. Housekeeping is a marathon, not a sprint. Go slow and steady. Don't start a whole closet if it is too much. Plan to do two shelves at a time if you can handle this better.

When you have done enough for one day, stop. Wait until tomorrow. Take one day off each week so you can look forward to a break. I also advise that you leave the kitchen until last. Kitchens aren't for rookies!

During my stint with the Mount Vernon Method, I sometimes came to a place I felt I just couldn't tackle. To get around this obstacle, I did two things: (1) I took an extra day off, and (2) I decided to reward myself with something extra special when I finished the "big bad job."

That kept me going!

When you are ready to start, make a list of several items —three to seven—that you plan to do each day before you start Mount Vernoning. Remember that the Method is for organizing, not for heavy cleaning.

Begin at the front door and start with the first piece of furniture you come to that has a nook, cranny, drawer, etc. As you move from one spot to another, take with you three boxes: a give-away box, a throw-away box, and a storage box. Open the first drawer.

Throw away every piece of junk that has accumulated there. Be serious about it. Don't keep the pen that only works half the time; toss the pretty calendar that's already a year old. Your freedom from clutter is more important than they are.

When you find things that are too good to throw out, put them in the give-away box. And give them away soon! You'll be glad you shared. Two cautions are in order:

1. Don't take anything out of the give-away box once you've put it in.

2. Don't wait for the perfect time or the perfect person to

give it to. Get rid of it right away. Don't save a matchbook for Mary's son who saves matchbooks. Don't even save it for a garage sale unless you have a specific date set for a sale. After that date, give it to the Salvation Army or Goodwill.

Be willing to take a risk that you may later want what you discarded. One Messie who is succeeding at becoming a good housekeeper wrote to tell me that the risk is worth it:

> I can honestly say that we have never missed anything that we got rid of. We did replace one ancient single bed which we sold and later needed. Cost was seventy-five dollars—a small price for the use of a room for three years. (The bedroom had been so stuffed with junk, it was unused until then!)

Remember that although it may cause temporary pain to throw something out, it also causes definite pain to keep it. Tossing it out is mild pain compared with the pain that comes from having to live helplessly with all that clutter. There is an exhilarating feeling of freedom that comes once the decision is made to take control of the house.

The storage box is there to keep the things that don't need to be discarded but are in the wrong place. Do not hop up and put them in another place while you are cleaning, because this will break your concentration. You may never return to your job there. Just put them into the box to be put away when you finally reach the place where each belongs.

It does not matter how quickly you complete the Mount Vernon phase. What matters is that you are consistent in your efforts and determination to complete the task. This does not mean that all I had to do to put my house in order was to apply some willpower. Not so! Over the years the willpower method had not worked any better than anything else for me. No, it required a *system*—and some very special tools.

11

Four Friends In Deed

Any Messie can tell you that the real problem of housekeeping is not getting the house in order; it's *keeping* it that way! There are four devices which together will keep your whole life organized. They are the *Flipper*, the *Box*, the *Notebook*, and the *File*. Here's how they work.

The Flipper: Magic Key to Maintenance

Doesn't that sound quaint — *Magic Key to Maintenance?* But there really is something magic about the Flipper: It works, and lists don't!

The Flipper is the heart of the Messies Anonymous organizational program. Many books on housekeeping say, "Make a schedule of daily activities for the house." Sometimes they then give a sample list so that you can get the idea.

Well, I used to make lists—usually at the insistence of my frazzled husband, who kept repeating in a comatose way, "Something has to be done."

Then I either put the list in a pile where it would be safe and lost, or I attached it to the refrigerator where I got so used to seeing it I no longer "saw" it and didn't miss it when it slid down between the refrigerator and the counters.

One reason I didn't use these lists is because I didn't really trust that they were good lists. I didn't respect them. Maybe they were poor lists. Maybe I didn't have every job listed and at the right intervals.

Then, too, the lists looked sloppy. They were handwritten and irregular, like everything I tend to do is. Who could respect a flimsy, messy, handwritten piece of paper that purported to tell me how to live? I resented that stupid list forced on me by grimy necessity!

But a system is necessary. One day when I was in the bathtub deep in thought, the idea of the Flipper dawned. Simply put, the Flipper is a three-ring notebook containing a series of twenty-four cards covered with plastic. The cards are arranged in a staggered series and attached to a larger heavier sheet of card stock. It is the type of system sometimes used to store and show snapshots.

You can flip each card up to see the one below. That's why it is called a Flipper. On these cards I decided to list information that would help me with my housework and menu planning. I stored three weeks of permanent menu plans on three cards and three weeks of daily household jobs like "make bed," "wash dishes" on three other cards. The rest are used to spread out all of the other household jobs that are not done daily (like mopping the kitchen floor) over a three-week period. Some are done weekly, some twice weekly, some every three weeks, and so on, depending upon the job.

After the cards are filled out to meet your needs, they are slipped into the plastic sleeves where they are kept in proper sequence and protected.

The net result is that you have, contained in your Flipper, a predecided plan of cleaning for each day and a menu plan for three weeks. Let me explain the highlights of the Flipper System to help you understand it a little better.

The Flipper System puts you on an easy-to-keep daily maintenance schedule. The house will not always be perfect, but with the Flipper it will always be maintained at an acceptable level. After I started using the Mount Vernon Method in conjunction with a few daily jobs from my own Flipper System, my house showed a remarkable change in only three weeks' time. It is important to realize, however, that you cannot use the Flipper successfully until you have "Mount Vernonized" your home.

Another nice use of the Flipper is the menu-planning system. It is designed to save time. I originally came up with the idea from something I read about Ethel Kennedy. She makes up two weeks of menus, goes through them, then starts again at the beginning for the next two weeks. That's what we do. But we outdo Ethel and plan *three* weeks of menus!

You might say, "Won't that get monotonous?" Not really. Studies show that, without planning, 80 percent of the time the same ten dishes are used over and over again. It is not easy to think of twenty-one different dishes—seven dinners a week for three weeks. You may wish to repeat a dish — spaghetti, hamburgers, or whatever your family favorites are — more than once during the three-week period. One day a week can be left open to take advantage of whims, gourmet recipes, or seasonal specials.

You can also change your menus every few months if you wish. Each week's menu is put on a separate card and stored in the Flipper. Now you have a permanent menu. From this permanent menu you can make a permanent shopping list— one for each week's menu. I don't know about you, but I hate to make shopping lists! Now we don't have to. Simply store the shopping list in the plastic sleeve on the back of the menu card and slip it out to take to the grocery store when you go shopping. Or, if you wish, you can put a duplicate page in your Notebook so you can have it if you decide to stop at the store unexpectedly (the Notebook is described later in this chapter).

One other convenience is possible with the menu plan. Let us assume you have some dishes that require a recipe. Instead of looking up the recipe each time, copy it and store it in the plastic sleeve above the day it is used. It will not only be readily available but protected from splatters, too.

For more information about how you can obtain a Flipper, see page 157.

The Box

Next to the Flipper, the Box is the most important tool in the organizational program. It would be easy to underestimate the value of the Box. Be sure to include it as part of your program. It will streamline your life and take a lot of pressure off the piles in the house. It is basically used for keeping records and storing information.

The Box is a wooden, metal, or plastic container that holds index cards. Such "recipe" boxes are sold in drug stores, grocery stores, and department stores; they can also be purchased in stationery stores, where they are called index boxes.

Although you may prefer to use 4 x 6 cards, I've found that 3 x 5 file cards work best for me. Along with your Box you will need to purchase one or two packages of file cards, a 3 x 5 scratch pad, some 3 x 5 dividers labeled *A* to *Z*, some dividers that are labeled with the months of the year, and some dividers that you can label yourself. These dividers will separate the contents of the Box into several main sections.

Address Book. The A-Z part of the Box will become your telephone and address file. Any number you call or address you use should be put into the file in the Box. Address books are hard to maintain. They get full; they need changing, so we cross out one address and put another over it. This looks messy. They become obsolete because of the changes. The Box file solves that problem because if a change needs to be made, the original card can be thrown away and a new card put in.

The Box is also better than an address book because there is room to make notes. Let us say you have a friend from college whom you never see but with whom you correspond at Christmas. You get a birth announcement from her. Write down on the card the name of the new baby and the date of birth. Then when you send your card you can write, "How is little Helen? She must be so cute at two." You can also make notes about friends' likes and dislikes in food, how their coffee is taken, and so on. They will be pleased you remembered.

Business Records. If it is a business call you make, you can make notes for that, too. I called Disney World and made a card for my file. I wrote down the prices they quoted to me and dated it. I will know where the price information is stored for use this year and will also have a record of how the prices change from year to year. It is filed under *D* for Disney.

If you have a plumber come, make a note about what he did and the date. Then if the same thing breaks down again, you can tell him when he was there previously and what he did. Keep records of car repairs and expenses under *C* for car.

Making notes in the Box is valuable for keeping track of orders you place. If you buy something by mail, write down the name and address of the company and the date you ordered it. If it does not come within a reasonable length of time, you can write, telling them how long it has been since your order. Put down the date of the inquiry letter on your card as well. In this way we can keep our lives under control by having necessary information readily available.

By the way, when you order by mail, put the address of the company on the back of the check to make it easier to write them if there's a problem. This has nothing to do with the Box, I just wanted you to know.

Newspaper Clippings. The A–Z file can also take the place of a newspaper clippings pile. Suppose you have an interest in restaurants and your local paper carries regular reviews of restaurants. Instead of cutting out the article, transfer the information to a card and file it under *R* for restaurants (see sample).

Restaurant

Le Flambeau
East Lang St.
Mon.–Fri. 11–10
Sat. & Sun. 5–11
#821-4620
Morn News: 8-5-81

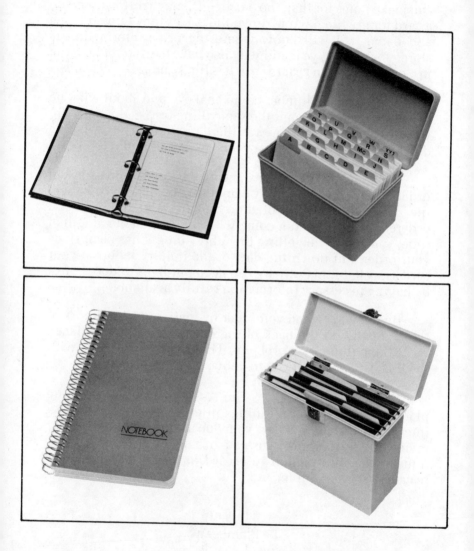

If someone recommends a book to you, write it on a card and file it under *B* for book. You'll have all the information summarized and at hand when you want it.

Monthly Activities. The monthly activities part of the Box is used to store reminders of activities that are done only seasonally or yearly. Check your monthly card at the beginning of each month. Let us say that you wish to turn your mattress four times a year. Behind January, April, July, and October put "Turn mattress in master bedroom." You can put notices to remind you to clean the gutter, store seasonal clothes, wash living room drapes, and other seasonal or annual things on the list of activities which you used for the Flipper.

You will also wish to list birthdays and anniversaries behind the month in which they occur so you can send a card or make a call for the special occasion. If the event is on November 1, put the notice in October.

Once you start using the Box you'll think of lots and lots of wonderful uses for it. If you have some short-term information you want to put in the file, put it on a piece of scrap paper and file it. Throw the paper away when you have finished with it.

Special Interests. The special interests part of the Box is for keeping information that is unique to your home and family. There are four or five blank dividers for that purpose. I use mine for storage information, like where I stored the Christmas, Halloween, or seasonal things. I use it for notes on a real estate course I took. I use it for records of special days, things like who came to the house on Christmas last year, what we had for dinner, and what gifts were received. I am sentimental, I guess. It makes me feel good to know one card per holiday has those memories safely preserved.

One person I know has a divider labeled *Health*. In that section she has a separate card for each member of her family. She records the dates of immunizations, surgeries, and so on, and details information about allergies.

In a section on *Finances* she keeps cards that contain all the insurance policy numbers for life, health, car, and fire insurance. She also records checking and savings account numbers and credit card information. Because her savings passbooks are exactly 3 x 5, she files them in this section. In the event of an emergency she has all her vital information at her fingertips.

The Notebook

The Notebook is the tool that will keep your *life*, as opposed to your house, organized on a day-to-day basis. If you try to organize everything in your mind, you'll become distracted and spill the details.

Mine is a small Notebook that fits into my purse easily and contains loose-leaf, lined paper separated by several dividers. Those calendars with little boxes for each day are too small for my busy life. I need a whole page for my daily "to do" list alone.

Here's how my Notebook works. Each divider is labeled, and I put information and reminders into the appropriate section. The divider labels are:

Goals In this section I write my life goal, ten-year goal, five-year goal, and yearly goal. Your immediate goal for a special project, such as your house, may also be written here. Recently I put my goals in the Box. Because my goals were so personal, I didn't want to risk losing my Notebook, and I was reluctant to have anyone else see them. I feel more secure about keeping them in the Box, but the Notebook is also a logical place for them.

To Buy Sometimes a special need comes to mind. While you are cleaning house you may see that you need batteries, light bulbs, rubber bands, and paper clips. I write these things here as a reminder. Whenever I'm in a store—even if I'm only window shopping—I flip my Notebook open to the "Buy" section to see if I need anything. This ensures that my house remains stocked with those little necessities that are easy to overlook.

To Do I make a different page for each day as the need arises. Then I make a list of necessary activities for the day.

Make sure your Notebook isn't cumbersome. If you make it difficult to use, you'll ignore it.

Now comes the important part: EVALUATE EACH AC-
TIVITY AND ASSIGN IT A PRIORITY. The really important
activity or activities will be *AA*. The important ones are *A*.
Next are *B*'s and *C*'s.

Now you can tell at a glance which tasks of a day are
crucial. Our tendency is to do the easy tasks, not the important ones, first. Assigning priorities solves the problem and
gives direction to our activities.

Any special interest dividers may be added to meet your
needs. I have a *Prayers* section in which I write prayers, and
Bible Study in which I write notes from the Bible reading I
do. If you have these interests or others you may wish to
include them in your Notebook.

A companion to the Notebook is a yearly calendar book
of the kind necessary for appointments and so forth. A few
frequently used phone numbers can be kept here for use on
the road. The full phone and address information is kept in
the Box, however.

File—Don't Pile

The word *file* conjures up visions of a large, steel gray,
office-looking thing which we don't have room for in our
houses and might not want there if we did have room. This
kind of file is costly, unsightly, and bulky.

But there are other kinds of files that are cheaper to buy
and easier to find room for. I suggest a Pendaflex-type of
hanging file for home use. It is made of heavy rods which are
fastened together, and it can be put anywhere. These are sold
at many variety stores, discount stores, department stores,
and office supply stores. I bought mine at Sears and was
happy to find one so short. They can be cut down to fit if you
find one too big for your available area.

Where will you keep it? A hanging file can be slipped
into any file drawer, either in a file cabinet or in the file
drawer of a desk. But the beauty of this kind of file is that it
can be kept in out-of-the-way places. Carmen, my Cleanie
friend, keeps hers in the living room in a decorative carved
wooden box brought to her by a friend who visited Ecuador. I

keep mine in an alcove in my coffee table where it is hidden by a door. You can buy one-drawer home files which take up little space and can be set on a counter without looking out of place.

The File should be used for storing larger pieces of paper or information that do not fit into the Box. Receipts, bills, clippings—these go into the File. Addresses and short notes to yourself go into the Box.

A File is a necessity for handling the papers that come into our houses. I suggest you take all your mail and either file it or throw it away at once. Even if you don't file it immediately, you can file it under "To Be Filed."

My mother has a ritual. She gets the mail from the box and walks directly to the trash can, sorting as she goes. In go the things that don't interest her. The problem with many of us is that we have trouble making up our minds what to throw away. If you walk right to the trash can, you will soon get the hang of it. It's a good idea to tear up any of the papers with your address or any credit card numbers on them so that no one will pick up the information out of the trash.

An excellent book that deals with files, among other topics, is *Getting Organized* by Stephanie Winston. The reading may seem tedious but it is worth making the effort to get the File working properly.

A word of warning is in order: Messies *love* files. From my seminars and conversations, I find that Messies frequently have not just one four-drawer File, but three or four! It is the one big attempt at organization they have made. These are storage files. These files are frequently kept in some out-of-the-way place and seldom visited. In business, a study has shown that 80 percent of the items filed never see the light of day again. My guess is that 90 percent of things put in a home storage file are never used again.

But isn't it satisfying to know they are there somewhere in case we should ever want to see them again? In a way, yes; in another way, no. Frequently these large collections in our Files are unorganized and difficult to use. In addition, the drive to squirrel things away puts pressure on us. As long as we have a File with folders, we feel an obligation to look in magazines and newspapers for articles to feed the empty spot. This means we have to read lots of magazines, we have to clip things out, we have to put them into the File. In the end *we* are working for the File; the File is not working for us.

If you have grown and cultivated one or more of these Files and it is sitting fat and full at your house, what are you going to do with it now?

I suggest you leave it until last in your Mount Vernon organizing. Could you, would you, maybe, in some wild dream, consider throwing out some of that unused stuff — *and* its manila folder, so you won't be tempted to refill it? And might it be possible by some strange and wonderful miracle to sell or give away the whole four-drawer storage File and get a little one- or two-drawer working File?

How do you keep a working File working? By virtue of its size, the small File forces you to keep only the essential items and to choose which items must be discarded. A smaller File can be kept close to where you do paperwork, and that makes it more available. Availability helps you to overcome the temptation to "leave it until later."

"But what will I do with the things I want to keep?" you ask, a little angry at my lack of understanding in this important area. Ask a friend whose home and papers are under control. Be sure this person is not a collector. The best way to see how to live without all this filing is to find someone who lives successfully without a collection file.

The more you discard unnecessary items, the closer you will be to having an orderly home—and keeping it that way. The four tools—the Flipper, the Box, the Notebook, and the File are indispensible, and I encourage you to use them or to develop your own version of them.

Meanwhile, it's time to tackle the hidden nemesis of every Messie. It's time to figure out what to do about those closets!

12

Closets

Don't you think it's wonderful when you go to see a Cleanie and she says, "Have you seen my house? Would you like a tour?" Then she parades you all through, even into the bedroom *and* opens the closet door! "This is my closet," she says. Wow! She even takes pride in her closets. And the closets reflect it.

Let me digress to say that the reason Cleanies show you around the house is because they consider the house an art form and they work at each part of their homes in the same way in which an artist paints different areas of canvas. As you work on the house, think that there might be a time when you will want to show people around your house with pride or at least take them to the bedroom closet to show them a new dress you have bought with the confidence that you will be proud of your closet.

Clothes Closets

What is the closet problem? Most closets are too small. However, if you look at your closet you will see a lot of wasted space, usually below the clothes and above the clothes rod.

The logical solution is to put two bars one above the other, thus making better use of more space in the closet. To put in two bars, the top bar needs to be raised. Carmen, my Cleanie friend, did this by taking out all the wood shelves and bars and replacing them with plastic-coated, ventilated wire shelving. There are three advantages to this type of shelving. One is that you can see what is on the high shelf more easily through the spaces between the wire. Another is that it requires less dusting since there is no solid shelf. A third is that if you wish to buy shelving without a bar, the shelf holds the clothes hangers apart evenly. The Sears catalog has a whole section on this type of closet.

There are closet companies that will do this for you if you cross their palms with silver. Look under *closet* in the yellow pages.

Now suppose you say, "That's too big a job for right now. What can I do with my closet the way it is?" Let me tell you my situation. If it requires a hammer and nails and takes more than five minutes to do, I don't do it. Neither my husband nor I are handy with building things and the few occasions when I have had someone do it for me have been unsatisfactory. So I look for easy-to-install ready-builts. In this case, add another shelf to the top of the closet with boxes and a board in order to make use of the empty space up there. Of course, that shelf will be pretty much out of reach so you should use it to store only seldom-used things. The unused space at the bottom of the closet can be utilized as a basket storage system. Look in department stores for suitable baskets.

An easy-to-install lower bar can be hung from the one above by two chains. Look in catalogs for this. A low bar in the closet helps the children get in the hanging-up habit, too.

Now comes what I think is the most chronic problem of the clothes closet—shoes. If they are left on the floor, even if they are on a wire floor rack with a hump for each shoe, they are unsightly, gather dust, and make it impossible to dust easily. There are several solutions. The one I am using now is the one Carmen suggested. I keep the boxes the shoes come in and stack them with the shoes in the bottom of the closet. I write in large letters on the outside of the box a description of the shoes. When I get my shoes out I leave the top ajar and the box pulled out a little so I will know where to put them back. It works well for me.

There are other good methods. The point is, don't let the shoes make your closet a mess. The back of the closet door is invaluable for storage of shoes, belts, ties, and some jewelry. If you make your closet a project (after you have finished the Mount Vernon Method, of course), you might get *How to Organize Your Closet* by Crislynne Evatt.

An important element of clothing storage that is often overlooked is the clothes hanger. Get rid of the wire hangers; buy plastic tubular ones instead. And have enough hangers. One reason people don't hang up their clothes is because it is so hard. Sometimes there aren't enough hangers. The wire coat hangers hook over each other, making them hard to take out. Frequently the wire hangers with the round cardboard tube given out by cleaners are broken in the middle of the tube when we get them out, which discourages hanging up pants. And then of course, there is the problem of too many clothes in the closet, which makes getting something in or out a tug-of-war.

Let me mention that you can pick up the plastic tubular hangers at many dollar-day sales, or buy a few each time you go to the store. Don't wait too long to get them, though. I suggest you paint your closet white and keep it that way so you won't have to repaint it each time you paint the bedroom. Buy one color of hangers; brown is good because it is stylish and somewhat neutral. Can you envision that beautiful neat closet with the white walls and brown hangers? Looks good, doesn't it?

The best color-coding application I have ever made is with my clothing. I divided my clothes into four groups: slacks, blouses, two-piece outfits, and dresses. In each group I arranged the clothes from light to dark like an artist's palette. This did wonders. Previously, I could not tell whether the pair of slacks I was looking for was out of the closet or in the closet, lost under something. Now I know that if my black slacks are not right at the end of the slacks section, they are not in the closet. This trick also helps me to see what clothes I have and how I can mix and match them. I highly recommend it to you.

Perhaps in no other area are we more tempted to keep unused things than with clothes. We have things too big or too small in case we gain or lose weight. We have things that are good but which we never wear because we don't like them. But they are *good*, that is, they fit and the buttons are on. So we *have* to keep them—especially if we paid a lot for them. We keep out-of-style things we used to love, just in case the style returns. It seldom does, and never in the same way. Sometimes we keep a dress which is out of style because the skirt could be made into something nice. We never get to that project; but if we ever do, we will have that wonderful dress to work with.

The worst reason to keep clothes cluttering up our closets is that we are keeping them in case someone else would like them. Sometimes we don't have a specific person in mind, so we keep them until we locate somebody who would profit by our generosity. Being perfectionists, we have to make sure it is just the perfect person. So we put the clothes aside until we get around to sending them to cousin Mary's boy. He'll probably have a son of his own before we get them in the mail!

Listen, let's quit dreaming. We are not going to do the alterations. We are not going to gain or lose weight while the style is still in. If we do, we can reward ourselves with new clothes. Don't wait for the perfect person to wear the outfit you are saving. Give it to the Salvation Army. Let *them* find the perfect person.

Utility Closet

Tangled extension cords, light bulbs, picture-hanging kits, these are the things that go into a utility closet. I have a super idea for solving that problem and I want to share it with you: Use clear plastic shoe boxes. I have about thirty in my closet. They are wonderful. When I first cleaned out the utility closet I found that the items to be put away were falling into categories. So I bought plastic shoe boxes (also frequently on sale at dollar days in variety and drug stores).

On the outside I wrote the various categories and put the groups of items in them. My boxes include:

- Shoe things (polishes, laces, brushes)
- Repair stuff (light switch plates, wall plugs, etc.)
- Curtain hardware (hooks for curtains, plastic balls for the pull cords, curtain rod brackets)
- Tape, ribbons, and strings
- Light bulbs
- Soap, toothpaste, and emery boards

Remember, the boxes must be clear plastic and the category must be put on the front either with plastic tape and a labeling gun or with tabs used for labeling in a filing system.

If you store mops or brooms in the utility closet, buy clamps and attach them to the wall. Awkward things like irons and ironing boards can be stored with special holders designed to keep them off the floor. Try to keep the floor as bare as possible. It's easier to keep clean that way and looks much neater.

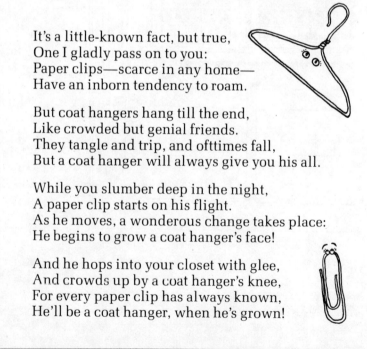

It's a little-known fact, but true,
One I gladly pass on to you:
Paper clips—scarce in any home—
Have an inborn tendency to roam.

But coat hangers hang till the end,
Like crowded but genial friends.
They tangle and trip, and ofttimes fall,
But a coat hanger will always give you his all.

While you slumber deep in the night,
A paper clip starts on his flight.
As he moves, a wonderous change takes place:
He begins to grow a coat hanger's face!

And he hops into your closet with glee,
And crowds up by a coat hanger's knee,
For every paper clip has always known,
He'll be a coat hanger, when he's grown!

13 The Kitchen

The general organization of the kitchen is very important. Things frequently used should be stored in an easy-to-reach place and near the point where they are needed. I found that my canned goods were near the dishwasher and my dishes were by the stove. I was amazed that I had violated the logical rule of keeping things near where they were used. I had to put the dishes closer to the dishwasher and the canned goods closer to the stove. I wonder if the most obvious rules aren't the most violated because we assume we will observe them automatically?

When I moved my canned goods I decided that color coding would be a good organizational trick. I put all my white and yellow canned goods first on the shelf with no regard to whether they are fruits or vegetables. I put my green foods next. Then come the red and orange foods and finally the brown ones. This saves me lots of time when I am looking for things.

I also color code my drinking glasses. Each person in the family has a different color. That way each person can use just one glass all day, and we can avoid the sink-full-of-glasses way of life. If people have a difficult time remembering which color is theirs, you can attach some meaning to the color. "Mary, your color is green because you are growing so fast." "June, you have the gold glass because you are so valuable and precious to us," and so forth.

But even with color coding my canned goods and my glasses, I came to the unhappy conclusion that most kitchens do not have enough storage space. One reason is that kitchens tend to collect too many unused items. Another reason is that there is a lot of unused space since the shelves are too far apart and several inches of space are wasted. Sometimes another shelf can be inserted to give more storage space. Wire rack shelves or wire hanging shelves can also be used to do the same thing.

The place under the sink is full of wasted space. It can be made useful by putting in shelves that avoid the pipe.

Hang-up Tips

I am becoming more and more convinced that Cleanies do a lot of hanging up of things without even realizing it. They do it to keep surfaces clean — but it also helps when there are storage problems. Here are some quick hang-up tips for the kitchen:

- Use cup hooks or an accordion coatrack to hang up cups.

- Use hanging baskets to hang up fruits and veggies. We had limes, avocados, and oranges that took up valuable counter space until I bought a hanging basket.

- Hang knives on a knife rack. It frees drawer space and keeps them from nicking and dulling each other in the drawer.

- Hang up brooms and mops. This gets them off the floor where they tend to fall over and clutter things. It takes the pressure off the bristles which can bend the broom and ruin it. You can buy holders for this purpose at the hardware store, or you can use a screw with an eye in the top of a wooden handle to hook on to a cup hook mounted on the wall.

The backs of doors are also very important for storage in the kitchen. You can put small wire shelves or racks for spices on the backs of doors. Racks made by Rubbermaid or other manufacturers for holding aluminum foil, bags, plastic wrap, soap and steel wool pads, and so on clear a lot of shelf space.

Cooking utensils can also be hung up, thus eliminating the clutter they cause in drawers. It is a good idea to hang measuring spoons on the back of a kitchen door on cup hooks. Hang pots on the wall, but be sure not to have so many things hanging around in the kitchen that it begins to look cluttered. Since shelf and drawer space are at a premium, hang or stand up anything that can be hung or stood up.

Shelves, Cabinets, and Counter Tops

However you arrange your shelves, you'll want to line them with an easy-to-clean liner. Use linoleum! You can buy it in smaller pieces at places like K-Mart. Less expensive than linoleum is Con-Tact paper. It is self-adhesive and lasts years. Drawers and cupboards are a pleasure to wipe out with a damp cloth.

If you've never used Con-Tact paper, you may find it a little difficult to handle at first. Cut to size first, leaving backing on. Tear off backing in one corner about three or four inches in diameter. Being careful that the corner is turned up so it does not adhere, fit the sheet exactly. Then place that corner down. Now the paper won't slip.

Start at opposite side and carefully peel off backing. Be sure sticky sides do not touch each other. Slowly slide your hand around so the paper spreads out and in place. Now lift the other end up—including the stuck corner—and remove the rest of the backing. Smooth paper into place. Many people have difficulty with their first attempts at laying Con-Tact paper, but with practice you can become adept.

If you have a kitchen cabinet with an open space above it, be sure to cover it. It will become really dirty and greasy, but the linoleum or Con-Tact will clean more easily than wood surfaces.

Kitchen cabinets do get grimy. You can clean painted ones with one cup of ammonia, a half cup of vinegar, and a fourth of a cup of baking soda in a large bucket. Clean greasy wood-finished cabinets by rubbing them with fine steel wool and paint thinner. Work in one area at a time, using long strokes.

Butcher block counters should be wiped with a cloth that has been wrung out with soapy water. Then dry the butcher block. Every two weeks, oil the top with mineral oil. Do not use vegetable oil, or it will become rancid. If your counter is made of formica, it will require very special treatment. Use baking soda to get stains off formica counter tops, and never use bleach or powdered cleansers.

Appliances

Refrigerator Helps. Use plastic grids made for holding fruits and veggies up off the bottom of the crisper. They save the vegetables from spoiling and they save on cleaning. Another good use for them is in the bottom of a self-defrosting freezer. The grids keep the food from defrosting while the refrigerator does.

Inside the refrigerator you can keep mildew at bay by wiping with vinegar. Don't forget to vacuum the refrigerator coils regularly. Some are under the refrigerator and some are in the back of it. Keeping the coils dust free helps the refrigerator work with less effort, giving you better service and longer life for the appliance. This kind of job should be recorded on your calendar or in the seasonally divided section of the Box. Remember also to clean the drip pan under the refrigerator regularly. Running it under hot water with a disinfectant, then spraying it with a mildew resistant spray will cut down on kitchen odors.

The Dishwasher. Automatic dishwashing powders can cause problems by stopping up the dishwasher with "gook." You can do several things about this. If it has been a problem to you, you might wish to try one of the dishwashing powders sold by private dealers such as Amway or Shaklee. These products have no fillers and therefore rinse away without scum.

In addition, set your water temperature to 140 degrees. (This setting will also prevent your clothes from becoming grayish.) It is also a good idea to turn on your hot water faucet for a little while to bring hot water into the pipes toward the dishwasher. Very hot water is needed to dissolve dishwashing powder and to keep scum from forming. Another trick is to run a half cup to a full cup of white vinegar through the wash cycle periodically to keep scum and lime deposits from forming.

Sneaking Up on the Oven

Nobody seems to know how long it takes to clean the oven, but most Messies seem to think it is a very long job indeed. Actually, it is not. Then why does it seem so long? It's because it is distasteful. The fumes, the goo, having to bend over in an awkward way. It's a messy job, so we think it is a long job.

Frequently, the more distasteful a job is, the longer we *think* it will take. This may or may not be the case. The only way to tell how long a job really takes is to time it.

What is the result of this kind of thinking? It causes us to procrastinate. We dread doing jobs we perceive as too long. We need to face the fact that sometimes we are just kidding ourselves. Some jobs are *not* as long as we build them up to be in our minds.

Some jobs, however, *are* long and hard, and we just don't get to them because they overwhelm us. They sort of hover in the back of our minds, draining off energy as they hover there.

In these cases, we have to manage a breakthrough to get started. The best method is to approach the job from its blind side. Don't let the job know you are really going to tackle it.

Let's take oven cleaning as a for-instance. First—make a commitment to do the job. In some place away from the kitchen where the oven can't hear, tell somebody that you are going to clean the oven or write it down as a commitment.

Second — get all the supplies in order. Buy an oven cleaner if you are out (I like Mr. Muscle), rubber gloves, and sponges. Read the instructions on the oven cleaner spray can. Keep the materials close to the oven but out of sight, so the oven doesn't see them.

Fortunately, oven cleaning is generally done in two parts, so your approach is already planned. You are ready for the attack. Now that you have made the commitment and actually begun, your mind knows that you are serious about what you are doing and it will begin gearing up for the job. Don't let too much time pass from this point on. Look for the first opportunity to do the deed. If you have a job outside the home, spray the oven and let it sit while you are away. If you stay at home all day, let it sit overnight. Don't plan to use the oven for the next meal because you probably won't have time to finish the oven before the next meal.

Now that the oven is sprayed, you *have* to finish it up. But by now your mind has adjusted to it. Besides, now the oven can't be used until it is finished so there is no turning back. So jump in there, wipe up all the goo, *put down aluminum foil*, and you're done!

In two isolated cases, people have told me they have no trouble keeping their ovens clean. When I asked, in surprise, why not, both told me they use lots of aluminum foil—to line the oven and to enclose food when it's cooking so it won't spatter onto the sides and bottom of the oven.

Three easy steps to a cleaner kitchen:

1. Outlaw snacking unless you're present. Then be absent from the kitchen as often as possible.

2. Feed all animals in the garage. Unfortunately, children don't classify as animals, for this purpose.

3. Eat out.

Helping
The System
Help You

PART FOUR

14

On Procrastination

An ounce of morning is worth a pound of afternoon.

What is that mysterious thing called *procrastination*? Why this chronic putting off of doing things when we know for sure that it is going to cause trouble later on? Why do we drop packages on the nearest chair instead of putting them away where they belong, put off paying the bills till they're late, toss clippings and mail in a pile, and leave the ice tray empty?

Like all things that have to do with human behavior, there probably are several reasons for this weakness which apply in some combination to each of us.

Probably the main reason we put off doing things is because we are not organized to do a job. Either we don't have a place set up for what needs doing, or we don't have a plan for handling it.

Akin to this problem is having a place or plan which is so hard to use that we just don't get to it. If our File is out in the garage we aren't going to use it; we're going to put our papers in a pile until we go out. That setup is asking for trouble. If we don't have enough coat hangers or if the clothes rod is jammed so close to the shelf above it that it is hard to get the coat hangers in, you've got a ready-made setup for procrastination.

We may put off the writing of checks to pay our bills because we really don't know how much money is in the bank. These are all organizational problems.

The more out of control a house becomes, the more there is to do, and the more impotent we become. On more than one occasion when my house has been in a total shambles, I have walked past a basket of clothes that needed folding and said to myself, *I really must get to that*, and then walked on.

The same is true of many other jobs, such as picking up a rubber band off the floor or filling the ice trays. In my case I was forever passing things by. It is because my housekeeping fuse was blown. Just as an electric circuit carries more and more electricity until it finally overloads and shuts down completely, so we keep going with more and more to do until our minds finally shut out what there is to do. It is almost impossible to get going again.

Thus procrastination is no mystery. It would be a miracle if a person did *not* put off doing things under these circumstances. Make it easy to do a job and you'll be much more likely to do it quickly.

Sometimes we procrastinate because we have let the job get so big that it has become very, very hard to do. One of the reasons Cleanies don't procrastinate is because they hate to do big jobs. They don't let big jobs develop because they know they won't want to do them and might procrastinate. In the case of some big job that can't be avoided, such as moving, plan to pack or unpack a few boxes at a time. Even though the job is big, we can set smaller, short-range goals and then we won't be so tempted to put off doing it.

I find that sometimes I put off doing something because I want the immediate gratification of some need. After a shopping trip, I am tired. I want to rest as soon as I get home. So I want to drop my packages, kick off my shoes, and lie down. I have reached the point now where the need to have an orderly, supportive home is more important than rest, so I am more likely to put away the things I bring in before I rest than to lie down and put them away later.

One of the most peculiar reasons for procrastination was one I noticed in myself after the change in my way of thinking took place. Somehow I had a vague feeling that someone else would do the job. Who, I do not know, but I definitely felt housework was not my job. Did I think I was an undiscovered princess, and the servants would do it? My favorite fairy tale was the one about the shoemaker who would awaken each morning to find that little elves had done all of his work during the night while he slept. Did I think little elves were frantically searching for my house and any day now, they would find it and surprise me? I don't know why I felt this way, but it certainly made me procrastinate.

There are other reasons for procrastination, such as lack of the clear-cut goal of having an orderly house. If this goal is lacking, it doesn't matter much whether a thing is done or not. Having such a pressured time schedule that we don't have time to do all that needs doing also encourages us to put off the harder jobs.

But there are other factors that influence our tendency to avoid the matter at hand. We find other things to do that are more appealing to us. Consider the following:

Reading: For bookworms, this is quite a temptation—a wonderful way of escape into another world which enables us to blot out the responsibilities around us. The piles around us grow dim as we lower our eyes to the book.

Daydreaming: Daydreaming, like reading, is a form of escape which takes time without showing results in the house. Sometimes we can use daydreaming about our house as an opportunity to set goals for it, but if we use up too much time daydreaming, what we daydream about never gets done.

Television: How easy it is to flip a switch and step into another world. Once I got hooked on a soap opera which became a problem because I felt I had to sit at home at a certain time for "my program." Housework faltered. Messies are particularly tempted by the TV Syndrome because it gives a certain order to the day. The coming and going of the programs helps us to pace our time. In addition, if we plan to watch a program and then do it, we feel we have accomplished one goal no matter how small.

Visiting: The desire to talk to friends is strong. We tell ourselves that friends are more important than the house. Hours of escape time can be spent on the phone, at a friend's house over coffee, and so on — and our time for doing the housework is gone even when we vowed we were going to "get to it" that very day.

Turning the phone off, leaving it off the hook, or just not answering it unless it is a special ring from someone you have a prearrangement with, are ways of cutting out this unplanned use of time. However it is done, cut down on talking time if it is a problem for you.

Leaving Home: One definite way of escaping housework is to be absent from home. Frequently too many social engagements, clubs, volunteer obligations, or shopping trips can effectively cut out the housekeeping chores. "I'm just so busy, I don't have time for housework." Sometimes extra reasons for leaving home such as making daily trips to the grocery store and ferrying children to too many functions cut up large blocks of time. Each one seems very reasonable in itself, until you add up the wasted time which you could have used more productively.

Perfectionism and High Ideals: Spending the whole morning cleaning the oven, ironing wash-and-wear clothes, overdedication to playing with the children, being meticulous about some small aspect of the house or your personal life to the exclusion of the truly important jobs which need to get done are just other ways of procrastinating. We're often trying to avoid the big jobs.

Sentimentality and Regard for the Old-Fashioned Ways: Baking your own cakes or bread, buying 100 percent cotton that needs ironing, doing windows the hard way, avoiding Mop & Glo or other shortcut products, mixing your own cleaning products, or collecting trinkets for display which need dusting are time-consuming jobs which are so unrewarding that we avoid doing them. Do you have some dusty pieces of clothing stored somewhere right now in a basket waiting for you to find time to iron them?

These are ways to escape from the *important* jobs we don't want to do. We do the easier jobs or more familiar jobs or the ones that we have to react to immediately because we have allowed an emergency to arise rather than setting goals and working toward those.

Stop and evaluate your use of time. Make a record for three days showing how your time is used. How much time do you actually allow for *planned* household tasks? You might be surprised that the statement "I don't have time for housework" is absolutely true because you make it that way.

How to Make Decisions

Another reason people procrastinate is that they hate to make decisions. Mary Beth was like that. Even going out to a restaurant that had a big menu caused her a lot of confusion. Deciding where to store things in the house or when to do a job overwhelmed her.

Mary Beth's problem is a common one. She had grown to feel that her decisions were not always the best ones. Mother would criticize or suggest changes to improve Mary Beth's work. She always urged her to do better. Consequently, Mary Beth learned not to trust her own judgment. It was less painful not to decide than to run the risk of making the wrong decision. As a result, she became a procrastinator. It was so hard to decide how to organize her closet that she just left it alone. Leaving it alone, of course, *was* a decision—a decision *not* to tackle the job.

This hesitancy to make a decision and to start a job is due to anxiety and a poor self-image. On the other hand, making a decision can be an opportunity to feel in control, to assert one's desires, and to enhance one's self-image. It is a way for us to control, rather than to be controlled by, life.

What is the solution, then, to the inability to make decisions? How do you resolve the problem of procrastination? Several suggestions may help:

107

1. **Narrow your choices.** Give yourself permission not to try to do everything at once. Let's go back to Mary Beth's problem of deciding on what to order at a restaurant. "I used to have that problem," her friend Esther said, "so I decided ahead of time on a pattern. When I eat out, I choose pork, beef, fish, and chicken, in that order. If I had fish last time I ate out, I know this time I'll choose chicken. It narrows my choices and makes my decisions easier."

2. **Predetermine many things.** The strength of the Flipper is this principle of deciding ahead on household chores.

3. **Set goals.** All decisions we make will move us in some direction. We need to determine ahead of time where we want to go. Then our decisions will be based on what we want to accomplish.

4. **Start!** The hardest part is starting because there are so many unknown decisions to be made, especially in a new activity. The reason that beginning is so important is because it is as we begin that we see what information we will need. We can also see how the job is going to be organized. Remember, "A job begun is half done."

5. **Ask yourself, "What is the worst that could happen?"** Suppose you are afraid that the decision you make will not be the best. Ask, *What is the worst that can come of this?* Frequently the answer will surprise you. The big bad decision isn't as big as you thought when looked at in this light.

6. **Be willing to make a mistake.** You are not perfect, and you will make mistakes. It is a part of life.

7. **Get information.** Lack of information makes decisions harder than they need to be.

8. **Clear the base.** When the house, checkbook, laundry, and life in general are confused, it is no wonder that we have trouble deciding about anything. When our house and our schedule come under control, we have a better view of what we need and how to get it.

9. **Take control.** The turning point in decision making will come when we adopt the attitude that a decision to be made is an opportunity—not a threat.

Once we start to make decisions, we will have greater control over our tendency to procrastinate. Procrastination is not some vague weakness in our personality; there are definite causes for it. Find the demon in your life that causes you to procrastinate, and you will find that procrastination becomes a problem of the past.

PROCRASTINATOR'S CREED

Knowing that procrastination is, at least in part, a matter of habit, I will do the following as a matter of breaking the procrastination habit:

I will make the bed as soon as it is empty.

I will fill the ice tray immediately and put it away.

I will put the toilet paper on the roll before it is half used.

I will clear the table, do the dishes, and clean the kitchen immediately after eating. I will consider clean-up a part of the meal.

I will put away what I get out and will not say I will be using it again soon.

I will put away my painting, ceramics, sewing, and other crafts when I am finished for the day, even if I will be using them tomorrow.

I will handle the mail as soon as I pick it up and will not leave it in a pile to consider later.

I will hang up my clothes and put away my shoes as soon as they are off my body.

I will be visually sensitive to anything out of place.

I will remember those three tender little words:

DO IT NOW!

which my conscience whispers when I am tempted to procrastinate.

15

On Making And Saving Time

Frequently we say we do not have enough time to keep house. This may be true in some cases. There are people who have so overscheduled their lives that they really don't have "enough" time at home to keep the house the way they would like to.

Aileen is one person who comes close to that state. She has a husband and handicapped son in the house. She works six days a week and on one of her free days a month she goes to the garden club.

That leaves only three days a month free. Such a schedule makes housekeeping very difficult. Yet despite that, Aileen is making real progress because she is following the principles of good time management. There are women who seem to be able to handle a schedule that is larger than life. For most of us Messies, however, it is wiser to schedule enough time to do what needs doing without Herculean effort. We are, after all, not superwomen.

When we say we don't have enough time, usually we have an organizational problem. We do have a few minutes here and there, but because we are not prepared with plans or don't remember what those plans are, the time slips by without our noticing. There are a lot of "little minutes" to be found between large blocks of time if we are just prepared to use them.

It is strange to think that the simple management of minutes can make such a difference in our lives. Actually it is at this point that Cleanies differ markedly from Messies. Cleanies value little minutes. They use little bits and pieces of time whenever they have them and consequently get a lot done without ever seeming to have to do long hours of housework. They do such things as clean the tub as soon as they get out, wipe the sink after they brush their teeth, hang up clothes as soon as they take them off.

The use of these little minutes will make the difference between success and failure. Success is very important to peace of mind and productivity.

A peculiarity of mine, and perhaps of yours, is the habit of thinking only of big jobs. If there is a little piece of paper on the floor, I say to myself, *Sigh! I guess I'll have to vacuum the floor,* and walk on by. My Cleanie friends would stoop down, pick up the paper, and the job would be done.

I think this idea of THE BIG JOB is a peculiar attempt at organizing on our parts. We react to the idea of doing a job rather than just doing the part that is a problem.

The reason for this no doubt is because we are "thought people," not "visual people." We would rather plan an activity in an orderly fashion and then do it (or maybe never do it; but at least it is neatly planned), than do a little bit at a time. Perhaps this is an attempt to stop the flitting around and distractibility that afflicts the Messie. But, like other good ideas that don't work, it needs to be abandoned.

Nevertheless, some jobs require a certain amount of thought and planning. Meal preparation is one example.

Cooking and shopping for food take a great deal of time. To speed up that process, plan menus and shopping lists for a week or so in advance. Sample menus and a shopping guide for one week are given on the following page.

Messies Anonymous Food Planner
Sample Weekly Menu

Sunday—   Baked soy chicken, rice, brussels sprouts, rolls.

Monday—   Hot dogs, sauerkraut, macaroni and cheese, sliced tomatoes.

Tuesday—   Spaghetti with meat sauce, mixed green salad, Italian bread.

Wednesday—   Fish sticks, baked potato halves, peas, slaw.

Thursday—   Cheese omelet, sausage, broccoli, biscuits.

Friday—   Tuna-noodle casserole, green beans, applesauce.

Saturday—   Broiled fish fillets, parsley rice, glazed carrots, rolls.

Weekly Shopping Guide
(Sample shopping guide for one week)

Chicken
Hot dogs
Hamburger (half lb.)
Fish sticks
Cheese
Frozen fish fillets

Brussels sprouts
Sauerkraut
Tomatoes
Broccoli
Green beans
Carrots
Parsley
Rice
Potatoes
Peas
Applesauce

Macaroni
Italian bread
Biscuits
Rolls
Noodles
Mushroom soup

Also:
Toilet paper
Cat food
Bread
Mayonnaise
Margarine
Laundry soap
Toothpaste
Bath soap
Dishwasher soap
Lunch meats
Lunch snacks

Also, look for easy-but-good recipes. I love the ideas in Peg Bracken's book, *The I-Hate-to-Cook Book; McCall's* puts out a quick cooking magazine; and there are many other publications at the magazine counter of the grocery store with the same emphasis. A recently published book you may want to look at is *Keep It Simple — 30 Minute Meals From Scratch,* by Marian Burns. Occasionally, bringing in take-out food will take the pressure off during a busy day. This idea loses its fun if it is overdone, but it certainly can be a help from time to time.

Double cooking is always a good idea. Make twice as much spaghetti sauce or bake two chickens so that another meal is basically started.

One of the ideas I like best is for the husband to take his turn at cooking. In my family, my husband is the head barbecuer. In Florida, where we have so much warm weather, this can mean a lot of barbecuing.

Don't let the family fall into the habit of eating at different times. This will wreck time schedules and is not ideal for family life.

Then, of course, there is always eating out. It, like take-out food, is nice for a change, but it gets tiring if overdone.

Question: What does the busy wife make for supper?

Answer: Reservations!

But our shopping needs are not limited to food. Consider how much time you spend shopping for nonfood and even for nonclothing items.

Catalogs save shopping time and energy. Sears, Penney's, and Montgomery Ward issue large, familiar department store-type catalogs. I like catalog shopping because of its convenience and because there are things offered in catalogs that aren't carried in the stores. You go from one department to another with the flip of a page. Ordering sizes has problems, but these usually can be worked out. Hard-to-get sizes are carried in the catalog, too.

Gift house catalogs carry many items I have found useful for organizing my house. Frequently the items, like storage shelves of certain types, are not easy to find in the store, but are staples of this kind of catalog.

Whatever you are shopping for, don't waste time while you do it. If possible, shop when the crowds are down. A full-time homemaker said to me, "It is a sin for me to grocery shop on a Saturday or a Friday night." If you can, avoid shopping on those days.

Everybody has twenty-four hours a day, but some people seem to manage those hours better than other people do. Consider how the following time stretchers could add minutes or even hours to your day:

1. Double up entertaining. Once the house is company ready, invite guests on two back-to-back days;
and/or
Have twice as many people over as you usually would. This makes one evening, one cooking, and one cleanup;
and/or
Have an open house for a very large number. Then you entertain many in one fell swoop, saving gobs of time.

2. Know where things are. How much time is wasted looking? Have a hook for keys just inside the door; have an eyeglasses holder; have a file for bills.

3. Plan for easy maintenance. Don't buy white rugs, clothes that need ironing, long-haired dogs, or knickknacks that need dusting. When you buy something, ask yourself, *Will it cause me work to maintain it?* Usually, because we are in love with the idea of how nice it will be to have an item and because we don't regard maintenance as very important, we buy what we like no matter how poor a choice it is from the maintenance standpoint.

4. Don't *do* so much. If you sat down and listed all your activities, you would probably be shocked at all that has crawled into your life while you weren't looking. Look at your schedule with clear eyes. Then begin weeding out.

Vegetables that are planted too close together jam each other so tightly that none develop properly. In order to have full, healthy vegetables, some good plants have got to go to leave room for the others. Some of us have so much jammed together that none of our activities are really producing well. The quality of life improves as the quantity of activities is reduced, if we have overscheduled ourselves.

5. Store things where they will be used. Store cleaning materials in each bathroom. Store towels in the bathroom, if possible. Keep the dishes by the dishwasher and the pots and pans by the stove. And know where they are stored. Nothing wastes time in a more frustrating way than looking for a lost or misplaced item.

6. Manage telephone and visiting time. If a lot of time is wasted talking, either in person or on the telephone, set your own time limits. If you clean house until 10 A.M., don't accept calls before then. If 6 P.M. to 8 P.M. is your time for the children, explain to the callers that you are busy and will call them back.

7. Move fast. In my interviews with Cleanies, I was surprised at the recurring comment, "I move fast," or, "I don't waste time getting it done." Cleanies want to get their housekeeping goals accomplished and move on to other things. As a Messie, I must admit that I took a more casual approach. One reason Cleanies move fast is that they have a definite time goal for the completion of their schedules.

8. Ask for help. In Proverbs 31:15, the chapter about the ideal woman, you will notice tucked away a mention of her maidens. This woman had help with all her enterprises! We need outside help, too.

We need a certain number of electronic maidens to help us with our work. Electric dishwashers, washing machines, dryers, microwave ovens—all can save time and energy in our busy days.

There is a point, however, at which too many gadgets become counterproductive, and we have to spend more time cleaning appliances and more space storing them than they are worth. In short, don't overdo in this area.

9. Buy time. Everybody has twenty-four hours a day, but there are different demands on each individual's twenty-four hours. If you have more jobs than time to do them in, buy somebody else's time. In short, get a maid or a cleaning service to help you. Don't feel guilty about it, either. You are not neglecting your responsibilities; you are just buying more time when you need it.

Unfortunately, a maid is not the answer to the basic problem. One woman said she had a full-time maid but still had a problem. The maid just kept her piles dusted. Another said her maid charged her ten dollars more to clean than she charged a neighbor, because the work at her own house was so much harder. Basically, you are the only one who can organize for yourself.

Then there is the problem of cleaning up for the maid. We would be embarrassed to have anyone come in and see the place like this. Some houses aren't ready for the maid yet.

Sometimes you can hire a maid to come and help with your organizational project if she is someone you feel you can work with in this way.

After you have developed your organizational system and have listed the chores for each day, you can give the maid the jobs of your heavy day and be free to do what you like. She is best used for maintenance. This is when she can be of real help to you.

It is tempting to try to use her to do what a maid cannot do, keep the house all week with just a one-day visit. You must follow your own daily plan of maintenance and break old habits if your house is going to look nice for more than one day a week.

If you decide to use a maid, the most satisfactory way to find one is through the recommendation of a friend. If you don't know anyone who can help you with a recommendation, ask around to find out how people in your area have found help.

But with or without a maid, you are going to need the cooperation of your family. In the next chapter, you are going to discover how to get the kind of cooperation you need without nagging (or at least without a whole lot)!

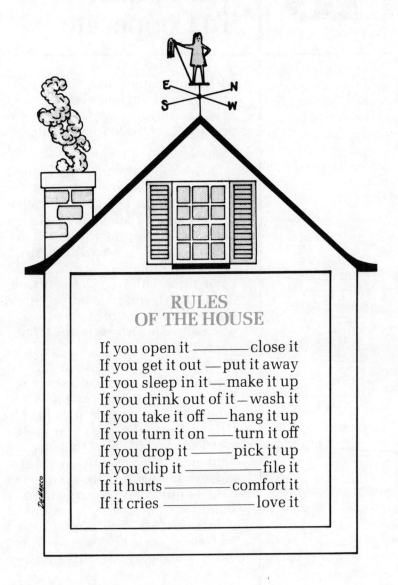

RULES OF THE HOUSE

If you open it ———— close it
If you get it out — put it away
If you sleep in it — make it up
If you drink out of it — wash it
If you take it off — hang it up
If you turn it on —— turn it off
If you drop it ———— pick it up
If you clip it ———————— file it
If it hurts ———————— comfort it
If it cries ———————— love it

16

Getting
The Family
To Cooperate

It is easier to rule a kingdom than to regulate a family.
JAPANESE PROVERB

If there is one place where your program will run into trouble, it will be with getting your family to cooperate. Read the following letter:

Dear Messies Anonymous,

The house is a mess now, and I don't feel very good about myself for it. I look out the window quite often to make sure no company is coming. One time I was in the mood for cleaning and my children said, "Who is coming?" Now that's bad! I have three children, ages fifteen, eight, and eighteen months. Since the baby was born, it really got worse. I wish I was very neat, but I am not.

Is it normal at all to have a messy house? I see some mess in my house and it depresses me. I am ashamed. I know I need help. My fifteen-year-old daughter helps when asked but even that doesn't help in the big mess. My eight-year-old son does not help, even when asked, nor does my husband. I should not have to ask. I should be able to do it all. But I don't. I know I will never win the "Tammy Tidy" award, but there must be a better way.

Please help,
M.F.

This lady's problem is typical. Let's be realistic. Just because you have a desire to live a different life doesn't mean the rest of the family is going to have the same desire at exactly the same time as you do. And you must realize that you may be largely responsible for the bad habits that have developed, especially in the children. Habits are not broken in a day, or in a week. It takes patience and determination within ourselves to overcome these obstacles. A big dose of humor and love toward our family is important.

But we should also develop a plan of approach. First, you will need to communicate your dream. Have a family meeting about three weeks after you begin your new program. You will have established your credibility by this time. Write out a goal-setting daydream to read to them.

You may also want to share the following letter with your family:

To the family of a Reforming Messie:

Someone close to you has become involved with Messies Anonymous. She wants very much to change her way of life so that the house is not a problem.

The decision to change is a significant one and she will need your help in that decision. Keeping house is a very complex job. The Reforming Messie is one who has become bogged down in that complexity but is not willing to live that way anymore. She feels a change is necessary—no, *imperative!*

The house is our home base. It is the extension of ourselves into our surroundings.

When visitors come unexpectedly and we are embarrassed, when we cannot invite friends over because it is too much work to prepare, when we can't find the important papers (birth certificate, insurance bill, income tax information, and so on), our way of life suffers and so does our self-concept.

And then there is the confusion. Why does so-and-so have such a neat and lovely home while I struggle and fail? Is there something wrong with me? If so, what is it?

On the other hand, when the house becomes neat, orderly, and beautiful not only on the surface but on the inside as well, a sense of control, confidence, and worth comes to replace frustration and guilt.

As the Messie begins to put this program into practice, you may notice some peculiar differences. There may be several responses from you to this change.

If you are a Cleanie—If you tend to be what we call a Cleanie (one for whom keeping the house neat comes easily), you may applaud what you see. All the confusion and clutter has been driving you crazy. At last you see a ray of hope. Let me encourage you to do what you can to help, but be patient and understanding. Now is **not** the time to take over and give all those hints and suggestions you always wanted to give. Don't rush things. The change must come from within, even if it comes more slowly than you would like. There may be slips backward that will discourage both you and your Messie. But remember, a detour is not a dead end. With encouragement things will get on course again.

If you are a Messie—If you yourself have the tendency to be a Messie, you may have difficulty adjusting to this new way of life. You may be a Messie who has frustrated yourself with this problem of messiness. You, like the Messie you live with, have been upset by this lack of control and the problems it brings to your life. Maybe you feel ready to tackle changing and join in the changing. For you the adjustment will be easy. You will be relieved. Or you may want things neater and more organized but may not be willing as yet to make any changes yourself to bring order. Or you may be one who says, "It doesn't matter to me what the house is like. I wish she would just leave things alone." What you need to realize is that having a nice house is very important to someone close to you and you have an important part in it.

When a person decides to change housekeeping habits, it involves the family in a way other changes do not. If a person decides to stop overeating, drinking, smoking, or the like, it is pretty much an individual endeavor requiring only encouragement and patience from the family. In the area of housekeeping, the family is much more involved in the change because the family functions in that house each day. The once easygoing Messie now becomes concerned if you get out the telephone book and don't put it away when you are through. Your shoes in the living room, once ignored, now become a problem. You may wonder if things weren't better before all this "wonderful" change started. Many times you will be **positive** things were better before all this neatness craze began.

Your understanding at this point is crucial. What the reforming Messie is undergoing is a new experience. For the first time, the house is a priority and for the first time she feels that there is hope. For the first time she is struggling with control in an area she has been defeated in before. When new things are attempted, it takes practice — for her to know how to approach you about the change and practice for you to know how to respond. So be understanding, be patient, and above all, be cooperative.

Change is always hard, but it *is* worth it—not just to the Reforming Messie but also to you. You will probably find after a time that you are changed and wouldn't want another way of life for the world either.

Love,
Mom

But communicating your dream will not be enough. "Many hands make light work." Translated into home life, this means that every member of the family must help with the solution since every member is part of the problem. In the book *Bonnie's Household Organizer,* there are four chapters that deal with getting children involved in the housework. Bonnie's new book *401 Ways to Get Your Kids to Work at Home* is great. Part of the reason that my friend Marcella's house is always nice is that her six-year-old has been well-trained and always puts her things away.

One way to do this is to put in writing every task that you want your family to help with. Then it is not you saying the job must be done; it is the written instruction which requires that the job be done. Writing, especially typing, is much more official than Mom. Mom's voice fades quickly and can be forgotten. Writing stays there until it is dealt with.

The Flipper will set up your household tasks in writing with a place for a check to show that the job is done. You can say to your son, "Jack, I want to mark off the job of taking out the garbage on today's card, but I can't mark it off until you do it. I really want to get this off my mind before I start dinner, so could you do it now?"

Don't forget to let him mark it off or see you mark it off, and don't forget to say "Thanks" as you do so. I have found people are amazingly cooperative when you are working with a checklist and not just telling them out of your own mind what to do.

In addition to communicating what you want, you must let kids know you are serious about what you have them do by checking it after it is done. People do what you INspect, not what you EXpect. Don't assume or hope that what you tell them to do will get done; inspect it and give praise or rewards for a job well and quickly done.

This is where many of us fail with our children. It is so much easier to assume they have done what they should without actually checking. And being distractible, as many of us are, it is hard to remember to check each time. But kids need to know that the job *will* be checked each time.

Finally, don't let the kids make a big mess. Kids can make a bigger mess than they can clean up. One reason we have a hard time getting them to clean up their toys—the tent made of sheets, the tea set out with all the dolls sitting around it, the pillows propped around for furniture, and the cookies, and the thermos with juice in it—is simply because it is too much for them to handle. It doesn't make sense to allow them to bring it all out and not make them put it back, does it? "You kids brought all this junk out and now you are going to put it right back where you got it. I want all that stuff put away before your father gets home. Now let's get busy!"

It is much easier for children to get things out of their proper places, to unfold the sheet and so on, than it is to fold the sheet and collect and wash the pieces of the tea set. Besides, now they are tired and their attention span is spent.

What is the answer? I frankly love to make a big mess. There is a certain wonderful freedom in living without restraint if only for an afternoon. I don't do it anymore, however, because really I don't want the problem of cleaning up a colossal mess or living with it if I don't clean it up. The "freedom" is not worth it to me. But because I know the joy of making a big mess, I tend to let the kids do the same thing, thinking I am doing them a favor. Then they are left with the problem I have learned to avoid in my own life. That's really not fair to them.

So the answer is to help the kids plan. You put some limitations on how much they can get out, where they can put it, how long they can play. They will want more things and time than you will allow, but soon they will get used to living less excessively and you will get used to directing them in a more moderate way. At first you will have more work to do because you won't be able to leave them on their own. I have noticed that children of Cleanies play more neatly than mine because the limitations on their activities were started earlier in childhood.

Be sure to tell your children ahead of time how long they can play, tell them ten minutes before the time elapses that they will have to quit and clean up in ten minutes. Then stick by that time schedule.

Behavior modification is another method to change sloppy habits of children. This requires serious thought to set up a plan for your needs. First decide what one specific habit you want to work on changing. Is it leaving toys in the living room, dropping books by the door, not making the bed, not hanging up the clothes? Work on that one thing and offer a reward for improvement. If there is more than one child, have them work together as a team. If the team succeeds in breaking the habit for that day, they are rewarded immediately. If one falls down, the team has to wait until the next day for the opportunity to achieve a reward. Be careful to encourage an upbeat atmosphere. Don't criticize the one who fails. Cheer success.

Remember you don't want to cause a mess in your family life while trying to straighten out the house. The house is for the family, so care is required to maintain love and good humor while making the change.

As in all things, love and patience go a long way in making the transition. It also helps to have some nice activity planned for them when they have finished with the clean-up.

Husband training is another matter, and I could not presume to tell you how to work most effectively with your husband. Each marriage is different and each relationship different. If you make housekeeping an issue between the two of you, you may lose more than you gain.

In my family I find the most effective method is to get the house in very good order; then things out of place stand out glaringly. Nobody likes to mess up an orderly area.

However, this is not always the whole answer. After twenty-three years of living with me, my husband had developed some poor habits, too. It is hard to say what he would have been like had he married a Cleanie. One day when I had concluded he was not showing the proper concern for my goals in the house, I decided to do what I suggest my students do: "If you have a need, talk about it."

So I talked, not in a grudging way, but in a way that expressed my feelings. To my amazement, my husband told me his view of how things were going and it made sense. I had not noticed some of the ways he had been contributing, and his heart *was* with me. Knowing this took a lot of pressure off my mind.

Sure, things go awry now and again. Sure, I have my weaknesses and he has his. But he lets me know about mine, and I let him know about his, we make adjustments and move on—usually in the right direction.

Perhaps you have tried talking but it made little difference. You might try *writing* how you feel to him:

Dear Hubby,

First let me say I love you. You have brought so many strengths to my life and to our marriage, and I really appreciate that.

124

I am bringing to you a problem that I have. For a long time I have been struggling with myself and with the house trying to get control over the clutter. And believe me, it is a struggle.

The only reason I keep trying is because it bothers me so much to live never knowing where things are or having to wade through so much stuff to look for something. It worries me that important papers may be lost in the piles. (I know they are probably there—but where?) I am afraid people may drop in unannounced. I want to be able to have guests over without having to go through Herculean efforts.

Most of all I guess I want to live in a beautiful house that I feel is under control. Perhaps you and I are different in how we feel, but I'll bet that if things were beautiful and under control, you would feel the same sense of joy I would and be proud of how the house looks. So I would like you to do two things:

First, I hope you will share with me my goal for a new way of life. Only if we stand together in this will we even begin to make any progress.

Second, I want to ask you to help by putting away the things you get out like ice cream bowls, magazines, shoes. Also I want you to help me clean up and get rid of the unnecessary things around the house.

It will be a big job and require a lot of effort from both of us, but let's do it together.

I can't wait until we have made the change.

Loving you,

Now you may expect any number of responses, from enthusiasm (not likely), to bafflement, to reluctance or maybe worse. Work with whatever attitude you get. If your husband's response is not satisfactory, have patience. Patience, I have found, is a big ingredient in marriage. Usually it pays off if it is born of love and commitment to each other.

Newton's law of inertia says that any body of matter at rest tends to stay that way unless some force moves it to get it started. Translated into housework, it means it won't be easy to break old patterns. Do as much changing as your husband will permit at a time, and you will probably find the going gets easier as you move along. It is not easy, but it is worthwhile.

How to get help around the house:

• Hide the kitten, then ask your daughter if it could be trapped under the junk in her closet.

• Tell your teenage son it's time his new girl friend was given an escorted tour of the house — including his room.

• Let your husband's socks lie where they fall until he panics at 6 A.M. one cold morning.

• Leave the dog's half-chewed bone where it is — between the bedroom and the back door — then wait until your husband has to let the dog out at 4 A.M.

17

More Tips On Organizing

It is my goal for all of you, and for me, too, that we should get and keep our homes organized in the least possible amount of time. I don't think it is unrealistic to say that our work can be accomplished in two or three hours each day. If you work and don't spend all day at home you will have less time and less energy for housekeeping. Nevertheless your goal *can* be achieved!

To accomplish this, a lot of cluttered surfaces need to be cleared. Special temptations for clutter are the top of the toilet tank and the bathroom window ledge. Kitchen windows, and kitchen counters, too, fairly beg to have things put on them: bottles, jars, tissue boxes, and appliances. The clutter turns any dream of cleaning these surfaces into a nightmare. There is no such thing as a quick swipe at the bathroom or kitchen in your morning cleaning when all these things have to be moved.

The best way to achieve order in the bathroom is to get a shower caddy and put the shampoo and conditioner bottles, the soap, and the washcloths on it.

In the kitchen, I suggest an almost bare counter. For a long time I fought this idea. I noticed that two of my Cleanie friends had almost completely bare counters. Still, I resisted clearing my kitchen counter because I thought it was an unnecessary and rather extreme step.

Then, in reading Anne Ortlund's *The Disciplines of the Beautiful Woman,* I again came upon the bare counter idea. That made it official! If it's in a book it carries more weight, so I tried it. What a difference it made!

Clearing my kitchen counter and color coding my clothes in the closet were the two moves that had the most satisfactory results for me. I didn't think either one was particularly important, but both turned out to be significant helps. I took the canisters off the counter and distributed them in several separate places in the kitchen cabinets. I put the blender under the counter in a place that had been cleared by throwing away some unused item. I felt I had to leave my toaster and my coffee maker on the counter, although my Cleanie friends keep theirs underneath. But since then I have gotten rid of my toaster, so that spot on the counter is empty. When my family wants toast, I broil it in the oven.

Now you are going to tell me that you don't have room under your counter. I know the problem. I am sure that men design kitchens and have no idea how much room is necessary for storage.

However, let me tell you of one woman's experience. She had her kitchen remodeled. During the remodeling, she put her kitchen equipment on a table on the back porch. After the remodeling was finished she decided to leave it on the porch and to get items to be stored in the kitchen only as she needed them. At the end of three months, half the things were still on the back porch. If you used this method, how much would be superfluous and left on the back porch?

I know the potato ricer belonged to Grandmother and the pots were Uncle Henry's, but you have the here and now to think of. Can you think of a way to clear out the space under the counter so you can clean off the top?

Another way to cut down cleaning time by changing organizational patterns is to plan not to let things get dirty. An ounce of prevention is worth a pound of cleaning up. Thus, you can put rugs both inside and outside the entrance doors so that dirt and trash will get caught there before being dragged into the house. You can put foil on the bottom of the oven so that if anything spills, all you need to do is change the foil rather than clean the oven. You can use cook-in bags for things that might splatter. If you don't have a cook-in bag, at least use a pot with very high sides.

One of the hardest problems for me to deal with was soap scum in the bathroom from the hand soap. It melts into the soap dish and foams over the side, hardening into semi-cement. I hate it.

Luckily, just at the time I was ready to do something about it, soft soap became popular. That was my solution. The only problem is that it is quickly used up by my teenagers. So when it is time for a refill I fill the container with dishwashing liquid. Sometimes I put slivers of bar soap in it together with a few drops of perfume. It works fine, making a perfumed creamy soap. This way, too, I can get rid of those pieces of soap that are too little to use but which I am too frugal to throw away.

Another method to speed up cleaning is to spot chronic problem areas and look for a solution. I had a trash can for throwing away food in my kitchen. It had no top because I thought it would be too much of a problem to remove the top each time, and it would be too difficult to do with scraps in my hand. The can was not very satisfactory because it was unsightly and the food kept splattering onto the white wall behind it, requiring frequent wiping with bleach and soap.

When I finally awoke to the fact that this was a chronic problem which needed a solution, I was tuned in to solving it though I didn't have any idea how I would do it. Soon afterward I was wandering through a discount store and saw a garbage can with a lid and a foot pedal that opened the lid. This kept the food scraps covered and when the top lifted back it protected the white wall from streaks and spots of garbage entering the can. I had seen these cans frequently but, until I had identified my specific cleaning problem, I had not really noticed them. If you identify a problem with a view to solving it, often the solution soon comes knocking at your door.

The final way to organize for order is to put things away. This is a very hard habit to get into, but it is a top priority.

I learned a little about this on the day after Thanksgiving. The shopping center was really crowded. The shoe store salesmen were bustling around. Shoe boxes and shoes were everywhere, some piled by the customer and some where the customer had been before.

There came a slight lull and the manager began clucking around the store, "Are these your shoes, Bill? Are these yours, Cal? Check these boxes—whose are they?"

When I asked him how he kept all these boxes and shoes straight, he gave me these tips:

1. Don't let too much time go by between straightening up. Keep things up.

2. Each salesman has his own area of the store for his responsibility so the manager has an idea who is falling down on the cleaning job when he sees what area is messy.

3. Every time a salesman goes in the back to get another shoe, he takes something with him whether it is his or not.

4. The fourth thing he did not tell me—I saw it. It was that he had his standard and he personally saw that the system worked.

The application to the home is obvious:

1. Keep short accounts — don't let things get too far behind.

2. Devise an easy-to-manage plan, so you can check on how each person is doing his job.

3. Everybody does his part and works as a team to get the job done.

4. We don't rely on the plan working by itself. We check on it and nudge it along. Remember people don't do what you expect, they do what you **in**spect.

These tips apply to all aspects of home management— even grocery shopping.

When you bring the groceries in, put them away, fold the bags, and either store them immediately or throw them out. No fair using the groceries out of the bag or, worse still, out of the car. You've got to put them away.

This principle applies to laundry, which should be folded and put away immediately, and to mail, which should be thrown away or filed immediately, too. When I write a letter, I put it in the mailbox immediately. So far it hasn't been stolen or rained on. Business executives, early in their careers, learn the value of handling papers only once. As executives of our own homes, we can apply this principle to our own work. Handle small chores as they come up; don't wait for them to add up to a mighty mountain of work.

But where and how do you get charged up for your work? Read on!

TEN COMMANDMENTS
OF HOUSEKEEPING

I Thou shalt not try to do everything thyself. Get help from children, husband, and maids as you can.

II Thou shalt have a goal, for without a goal, nothing will be accomplished.

III Thou shalt have a plan and stick to it.

IV Remember the family to treat them in love while you (and they) are changing.

V Thou shalt not over-schedule and thou shalt not say yes to everyone who asks. Set your own priorities and say yes or no in line with them. Take control of your activities.

VI Thou shalt dream and keep dreaming until your life-style fits the dream.

VII Thou shalt reward thyself for jobs well done and milestones met.

VIII Thou shalt make housework easy to do by organizing for efficiency, because only as work is easily done, will we do much of it.

IX Thou shalt find joy in beauty and order. We are not accomplishing these goals only for utilitarian purposes. Only as we joy in our accomplishments will we be willing to continue.

X Thou shalt not procrastinate. Keep things up and do jobs as soon as thou shalt notice they need doing. Do not leave it out to be put up later.

18

Energy: The Spark Plug Of Housekeeping

In the book of Proverbs (31:17), Solomon continues about the ideal woman, "She girdeth her loins with strength, and strengtheneth her arms." Apparently this woman knew some way to strengthen herself deliberately. There are ways we too can find energy to do our work.

As we work we can conserve what energy we have by wearing comfortable shoes, such as nurses or waitresses wear. If you work outside the home, make sure you do all you can to arrive home at the end of the day as strong as possible. If you must stand in one place all day, buy a spongy rug to prevent tiredness of the feet and legs. If possible, use air conditioning or bring your own fan if circumstances allow.

While I am teaching math classes in our junior high school, I use only a fan when it is not *too* warm because the air conditioner makes it necessary for me to talk louder which exhausts me. Instead of standing to write on the chalkboard, I sit on a stool and use an overhead projector on which I can write without moving from my stool. This has the added advantage of permitting me to face the class while I write, so I am able to keep an eye on my students while the overhead projector reflects the work on the board behind me. This is how I solve some of my energy-draining problems. Can you think of adjustments you can make to save some of that hard-gotten energy?

Another source of energy is nutrition. My daughter's miniature horse, Wild Thing, lives in a fenced-off section of our yard. When we first got the horse she had been eating sweet feed, a high-energy food. The veterinarian recommended that she should be switched to rolled oats because sweet feed gave her too much energy, and that would not be good for her in the somewhat confined area in which she lives. If rolled oats had proved to be too energy-producing we could have switched to horse pellets, which provide even less energy.

I am not suggesting that you should buy sweet feed. I am suggesting that the same principle applies to people. Find that combination of food that works to make you feel your best. Don't think it will come naturally; it probably won't. You'll have to search for the proper foods.

I have friends who claim that if they miss their vitamins one day, they feel a letdown the next. If vitamins help you, don't neglect them.

Medicine prescribed by a doctor for a special condition should not be overlooked. I take thyroid medicine because most of my thyroid has been removed and what is left should remain dormant. If I were to forget to take the medicine for any length of time or get the idea that I could exist without it, I would be a basket case before very long. Take health seriously, for the sake of your house and yourself.

Perhaps the quickest way to get a surge of energy is to improve your looks! A good haircut at frequent intervals is a must for me. I have heavy hair which tends to be oily. If I let it get long, it becomes heavy and droopy. Then I begin feeling heavy and droopy, too.

Another quick improvement can be made in the area of makeup. I go to Merle Norman shops because they are the only shops I know where people will carefully advise me.

Better department stores have cosmeticians who will help, but I feel a bit uncomfortable sitting on a stool in the middle of a department store, putting on makeup.

A warning is in order, though. Cosmetics are expensive and it is a good idea to go with some spending limit in mind. Buy a little now and go back for more later if necessary. Let me also recommend the book *Color Me Beautiful,* by Carole Jackson, as a guide to help you decide which colors will set you aglow.

Since my house has been organized, my mind has cleared up, too. Now I can give attention to details such as jewelry. I don't dress up every day using accessories, but I am happy to have the right ones when I need them. Previously, things were in such a jumble I had trouble knowing what I had or how to find it.

For those who spend the day at home, there is a temptation to bum around in the same old junky outfits. Buying a new outfit or two will put pep in your step. Getting up early, showering, dressing, putting on some makeup and a new smock, a shorts outfit, or whatever you find best to wear for comfort at work, will get the day off to a good start. Dragging around in a gown and robe telegraphs to your body that you really are not ready to work yet. The book *Dress With Style*, by Joanne Wallace, can show you how to add zip to your looks at home and out. So dress with purpose!

Above all, DON'T GO BACK TO BED! Sleeping is a temptation because it helps one to forget about the things to be done.

A long-range change in your weight will also produce energy. Too much or too little weight will wear a person out. It also discourages improvement of any kind in some people. Weight Watchers, Overeaters Anonymous, 3D, or several other organizations are groups to turn to for help. The first two can be found in the phone book if there is a group in your city; 3D is a Christian group that works through churches of all denominations and can be reached at Diet, Discipline, and Discipleship, Inc., 2710 Chili Ave., Rochester, NY 14624. Undoubtedly there are other groups around the country which could help you with your weight if that is necessary.

There is one organ of the body which has a great reservoir of energy waiting to be tapped. That organ is the brain. Have you ever noticed that when there is work to be done the body becomes very tired, but if there is fun to be had energy seems to come from nowhere? Having a messy house is tiring. William James said, "Nothing is so fatiguing as the eternal hanging on of an uncompleted task." He was right! Having all those odds and ends to do makes the day look like an unpleasant mountain to climb. Energy will come from order, and from success in gaining control of the work in the house. You will be buoyed by the order and beauty around you.

Success brings more success, and that brings energy. Three weeks after one of my students started on the program, her husband sent her flowers with a note saying, "The house looks great, Honey!" What do you suppose that did for her energy level?

Remember, too, that we all need breaks to keep our energy high. Some of us spend so much time trying to bring order out of the chaos of our houses that we don't take any time off for relaxation. We don't feel it is right to play until our work is done. And our work is never done.

Take one day a week for fun. Plan not to work on that day. Then when you get back to work, you'll get a lot more done.

Spiritual faith is another source of strength. In the book of Isaiah we read, "He gives strength to the weary and increases the power of the weak....those who hope in the Lord will renew their strength. They will soar on wings like eagles; they will run and not grow weary, they will walk and not be faint" (Isaiah 40: 29, 31 NIV). I really feel that much tiredness in housekeeping is tiredness of life as it is. Only if the soul is joyful can the problem be overcome.

An important habit to break is the soap opera habit. The people in these shows are losers — interesting losers, but losers none the less. They are immoral, too, and this is bad input for anybody.

I mentioned earlier that I was once hooked on a soap opera. I say *hooked* because I had to structure my day around the soap opera. I could not go out to do errands if I could not get back in time for the program. In short, I found I needed my daily "fix" or I was uncomfortable and hard to get along with.

Then the program was moved to a time when it was not possible for me to watch TV. What an answer to my need! I vowed never to get into that kind of bondage again.

One part of the program I did miss was the beautiful house the characters lived in. The folks were wealthy and had maids. One of the few spots of order and beauty in my life was that soap opera. Now it is much better to have order and beauty in my own house.

Good books of the right kind can be motivating and uplifting. But they, like television, require that you take time from your work. So use them sparingly at first if you are inclined to be a book addict.

Reading the Bible or another spiritual work first thing in the morning can lead us into that right relationship with the Lord from which we draw strength. If you don't know where to start I suggest the Psalms and the Book of John. From there you can branch out on your own.

We have decided. We have organized. Now we have time to paint a few dreams.

When I was younger, the house
    was cleaner,
As I got older, the dirt got meaner.

The babies came—they're all
    such joys,
And each one owns a thousand
    toys.

They begged us just to get one cat,
A gerbil and dog soon followed
    that.

Each teen brings home at least
    one friend,
The dirty dishes just won't end.

Yet soon our chicks will fly the
    nest,
Our house will shine, like all the
    rest.

I'll love it when you make a mess,
Because the messy years are the
    best.

The Payoff

19

Painting on Your Clean Canvas

The nice thing about being organized is that it enables you to do what you want to do, to paint what you want on your nice, clean, prepared canvas. This is particularly important for your personal life whether you live alone, with someone else, or in a family. Now you have time to establish your family or individual traditions.

If you are single you may think this section is not for you. Tradition is for families, right? Poppycock! I think tradition is even more important for singles to attend to than for families, because in families you have tradition more or less thrust on you by the kids or by your spouse.

If you are single, you are pretty much responsible for your own traditions or lack of them. Some people can carry on traditions for their own sakes. I can't. If I don't have someone to share it with I hardly think it is worthwhile. So I would have to build people into my tradition if I were single. They might be other singles like myself, senior citizens, families, or students.

I knew a single college librarian

who regularly invited students to her room for waffles. She had coconut waffles, pecan waffles, all kinds of waffles and syrups. A touch of home cooking meant a lot to us. Students would bring back special waffle toppings from their vacations. I am sure her life was enriched by her tradition. And so was ours.

If you are single, don't let what could be very rewarding traditions slip by because of lack of thought.

If you live near your family, many of your traditions will involve them. But don't settle for that. Be imaginative! Start your own!

With families, traditions are lying around for the taking. Bedtime stories, special foods, birthday parties, and holidays can hardly be avoided.

The problem with traditions is that they require a lot of effort. You have to be organized to keep a good tradition running.

If you put the system in this book to use, you will have a handle on things. You will know where the Christmas things are; you will know where the Halloween things are. In short, things will be under control.

You will be surprised how knowing where things are can enrich your life. Somehow it gives starch to the mind. Flabby, half-formed ideas will march out in full dress uniform for your family to enjoy. Things that were just too much bother will be done because now you will have the time and energy to do them.

What are some of these traditions? There are the usual things like displaying the flag on holidays now that you know where the flag is, and there are bedtime stories now that you have all the children's books gathered together.

Special foods from your own ethnic background or traditional family favorites are important. In my family we eat black-eyed peas on New Year's Day and believe the more peas a person eats the more money he will get.

142

A friend of mine adds a unique twist to this tradition. In her family they add a clean silver dime to the dish containing the peas. Whoever gets the dime gets double luck in the new year. They use the same dime year after year.

Then there are birthday celebrations. In the birthday cake you can bake a peanut. Whoever gets the piece with the peanut gets a special prize. Let the birthday celebrant be the one to select the menu for that night.

Recently we have added another aspect to birthday celebrations. At the table we each tell what we most appreciate about the person whose special day it is and then we give him or her a Bible verse.

Thanksgiving and New Year are at the beginning and end of the big holiday season of the year. I think Thanksgiving is my favorite holiday because it is, for me, a purely personal relationship between me and God couched in the context of national Thanksgiving.

It is a good thing that this refreshing holiday comes first, giving strength for the days to come up until New Year. But of course Christmas is the highlight of the season for us as a family.

You really have to be organized to have a satisfying and joyful Christmas. First you have to know where the Christmas things are stored. Hopefully they are all together in boxes labeled "Christmas" and stacked alphabetically in the garage, basement, or attic. But if they are not, you should have the places where they are stored listed in your Box under the special heading "Storage" so that you can find them when preparation for the big day comes.

Buying presents, putting up decorations, and cooking are the big three of Christmas celebration. Gift buying is best handled by spreading it out through the year so that by the time December 25 comes you are ready.

It is also a good idea to wrap each gift as you buy it so that you are not hiding in the back room on Christmas Eve wrapping gifts by yourself when it would be nicer to enjoy time with the family in the living room. Put the names of the people for whom you are going to buy gifts during the year in the monthly section of your Box at the beginning of the month in which you plan to buy them.

Decorations come out from year to year and carry more importance because of the memories tied in with them. The star you lifted three-year-old Johnny up to put on the tree is now put up by Johnny because he's the only one tall enough to reach the treetop.

Christmas tree balls are the most important of decorations. One of the saddest experiences of my early married life was the first Christmas my husband and I spent together alone. When the time came to put up the tree, a little blue table-top one, we had to go out to a store to buy decorations. There they dangled, strange Christmas balls, hung by string instead of metal hooks, since I fancied we were too poor to buy metal hooks. As a result of that experience, I decided my kids would have their own Christmas balls, with heavy tradition attached, to take into their own homes.

So each Christmas I buy four matching balls. One ball is for my husband and me to keep. The other three are for each of our three children. If possible we mark the year in an unseen place on the ornament and include the name of the child if it is hard to tell one ornament from the other. Some of them were made by the children at nursery school. Some we painted on summer vacations at the cabin. I guess it is too much to hope that the young people our children marry will bring a similarly collected selection of Christmas ornaments to be merged on the tree for their first Christmas together.

By the way, we still come across a Christmas ball now and again with a string attached instead of a metal hook. So even that first sad experience became a Christmas memory of the bittersweet kind.

Christmas foods tend to run in families. A special kind of turkey dressing, a favorite eggplant casserole, all are happily anticipated before they are actually enjoyed.

For a great book on Christmas get *Take Joy*, by Tasha Tudor. When you open the book you can practically hear the jingle of sleigh bells and smell the Christmas cookies baking.

It has songs, recipes, and best of all, loads of tradition. And when you have your house clean and neat, your storage under control, and your time planned, you can enjoy these traditions too. I bet Tasha Tudor is a Cleanie. One of the nice ideas she suggests is the Kris Kringle tradition. In her family around December 12, they each draw a name of a family member secretly. During the days between then and Christmas it is the Kris Kringle's job to do nice little things in secret for his or her special person. On Christmas Eve each person tries to guess who his Kris Kringle was and the secret is revealed.

Some of the hardest things to manage are children's treasures. These are papers, awards, school pictures, and other memorabilia your child brings home. Where can they be kept? The answer is a Treasure Box. This is a box about orange crate size which you can cover with sticky, plastic paper like Con-Tact. Inside put manila file folders—one for each year. If you like, you can decorate the outside with the child's picture and name. In each folder put some of the school papers from each year along with certificates and other mementos. There is also room for some of the bulkier treasures of childhood like the box with the frog skeleton.

Don't overdo. A sample of each thing will be enough to prod the memory.

In the regular flow of family life some nice everyday traditions can develop now that the house is not holding you back. For example, we like to have family night from time to time. For us it is usually a Friday night. A friend of mine could not come to a meeting one Saturday because she and her husband and teenage son had planned a family day for that Saturday. I like that.

I was talking to my daughter about our family traditions which had plugged along enthusiastically if not efficiently during my Messie years. She enjoyed the ones I mentioned, but she was really enthused about our traditional church activities.

I realize that not all churches provide the same support for the individual and family in spiritual and social ways as ours does. Our church is a kind of extended family, and the people are warm and genuinely interested in each other. They contribute a lot to our family.

It is important for us to get up and go to church. On Sunday morning, I like to keep the same schedule of popping out of bed, doing the dailies, eating breakfast, and getting off, leaving the house tidy in case somebody should come home with us.

If it is too much effort to make a big breakfast, have sweet rolls and sausage served on paper plates and let the children drink out of plastic cups. Throw the plates and cups away after use and you are ready to go.

From my personal standpoint, the Sunday morning church service is the highlight of my week. And it is much easier to go and really enjoy it if the house is in order and ready to send me off and welcome me back. It leaves me in a good frame of mind so I can relax and enjoy the day. Because I feel good about the order that is around me, I feel good about myself, and I am able to look forward to the fresh, clean canvas of a new week.

FAMILY TRADITIONS

Old Christmas decorations are the prettiest. New ones picked out or made by a child come next. Plastic ones fall short, unless they carry the baby's toothmarks.

For boys, enormous gift packages are the best. Middle-sized ones that rattle come next. Anything that looks like it came from a clothing store doesn't count.

For girls, tiny boxes from the jewelry store are best. Middle-sized ones that rattle come next. Some years, even boxes from the clothing store count.

The Fourth of July needs a parade and a cookout. It doesn't need rain. It definitely doesn't need the thought of Summer School.

20

The Real Beginning For You

You now know just about everything I know about how to leave the morass of messiness for an ordinary life.

I struggled for twenty-three years to play the housekeeping game, and for twenty-three years I lost. The methods I have shared with you have changed my life. They can change yours, too, if you choose to put what you have learned into action.

First, recognize that you are a Messie but that it is not necessary to live like one. It is possible to move up the scale. Commit yourself to becoming a 5, a 6, or a 7, and then analyze yourself to see just exactly which habits are creating the most difficulty for you.

Next, set some short- and some long-range goals for yourself, and then use the Mount Vernon method to organize your home. Be sure to discard everything that isn't useful or beautiful. Take your time and save your energy, because the changes you are about to undergo will revolutionize your life.

Once your house is organized

and free of the accumulation of the years, purchase the necessary tools to keep it that way—a Flipper, a Box, a Notebook, and a File. Always remember that procrastination can defeat you, and use your tools as effective weapons against it.

Involve your family in your endeavors and remember that it may take them some time to adjust to your efforts.

The plan works. It works marvelously, but only if *you* make it work. You must sprinkle the magic dust. I'd love to hear from you to know of your successes.

Good luck, and may God bless you as you begin to set and accomplish your goals. As for me, I have to go and dust my fuse box. A dusty fuse box is an unhappy fuse box.

Appendix:
Ideas That Work—
Motivating Yourself

Inspire Enthusiasm —Have one or two things in your house that focus your interest and enthusiasm—like a shiny toaster, a sparkling bathroom, or whatever fuels your energy.

Do It for Others —Invite company over regularly. Nothing helps you to see what needs to be done better than knowing that guests will come and see your house from a fresh perspective. We tend to see the house from their standpoint when we know they are coming.

Get a Maid —Consider professional help. Wouldn't it be nice, *after* you have gotten organized, to have a maid come in and give the house a special cleaning? If you stay home while she is there, you can tackle some big job you haven't had time for and *really* have the house sparkling.

Switch Jobs —Mop the floor of a friend and have him/her clean your stove. Somehow it isn't as hard to do someone else's house.

Have a Cleaning Party —Have a friend over to sit with you and talk, or to help you, when you are cleaning or doing a special task like organizing a closet. The friend will help encourage you to throw things away. ("Will I need this, Jane? Naw, probably not, I'll throw it away.") Then stop long enough to put things away. Go out to lunch together or go eat the special lunch you fixed the night before to celebrate.

Work With a Time Limit —Do a job by time. Set the timer on your stove, or better still, put on a record. Plan to work for only two or three songs. You may find that once you start you'll go on for a while longer.

If you have a big job, put on a Marine Band album or the "1812 Overture." That will give you enough time and enthusiasm for a huge job.

Give Yourself Rewards— Reward yourself for a job well done. Food is a good reward if you're skinny. Even if you're not, there are some very good foods, like artichokes and crab meat, that are real treats and not fattening. A piece of jewelry, a day with a friend, or an extravagant soap will do nicely.

Let One Success Lead to Another— Success is the biggest motivator. Once things are under control, beautiful, and convenient, you will not want to return to the old way again. The compliments of family and friends are the fuel that fires our minds, hearts, and bodies. And then there is that bottom line. We like the new way better ourselves.

Still More Tips for Organizing

Several sensible ideas will keep your house moving in the right direction:

One Room, One Purpose—Make it a point to use each room for the function for which it was designed. This means don't take off your shoes in the living room and don't eat in the bedroom. Plan to eat in the dining room or kitchen and undress in the bedroom.

Stand It Up—There is more air space than surface space, so it is a good idea to stand up anything that can stand up rather than lay it on a table, desk, chair, or sofa.

This is particularly true of magazines. If you have several special issues, make a magazine holder from a cereal box. Cover the cereal box with wood grain Con-Tact paper. It will look like a library box. Then place the magazines in it and put it on a bookshelf so that magazines are standing up instead of laying down.

If your drawers are crowded, consider hanging up your nightgowns or anything that can be hung up. This is the same principle in a different form.

Automate — If you know of any automatic products, use them. Some examples are fertilizer spikes which fertilize the plants so you don't have to do it so often. Some new cleaners that you can put in the toilet tank, not the old types that turn the water blue, clean the toilet automatically. Use anything that will lengthen the time between essential jobs.

Finally, START EARLY. For most people an ounce of morning is worth a pound of afternoon.

Also remember:

Early to bed, early to rise,
Makes your house neater than otherwise.

It's this attitude that gets most Cleanies off to such a good start in the morning. So get up, get dressed, and get going.

General Hints

Ring-Around-the-Collar— Use shampoo on collar and cuff rings. Shampoo is meant to clean body oil, which is what that ring is.

Window Cleaning—Use a squeegee and water spray. This is the easiest way. Also use a squeegee on the walls of your shower. It will keep water spots and soap deposits from building up.

Keeping Up With Things—Are you forgetful? Do you leave things lying around? Write your name, address, and phone number on all your small notebooks and other easy-to-lose possessions.

Vinyl—Don't put oil on vinyl to make it soft and shiny. It will eventually harden it and cause it to split. There are good vinyl protectors on the market. Grocery stores, drug stores, and auto supply stores carry them.

Storing Sheets—When you fold your sheets, fold the sheets and the pillowcases in one bundle, with the flat sheet covering them all. Then you can grab the whole set to be put on the bed with one hand.

Bathroom Fixtures—Use liquid cleanser on bathroom fixtures because powdered cleansers dull the finish. If you have a very dirty sink or tub and feel you must use a powder, use Dutch Cleanser, Zud, or Bon Ami, since they have milder abrasives than most.

Leftovers—Put a list of leftovers on the refrigerator door. Cross them off as they are used.

Plastic Ice Trays—Don't wash these in warm water. You will remove something that keeps the ice from sticking. If you have already washed them in hot water, spray lightly with Pam to restore the slick surface.

Waxing the Bathroom—You can use wax like Turtle Wax to polish and wax bathroom fixtures (not the inside of the tub, please). You can also use Pledge or other furniture polish to wax the ceramic tile if you wish. Just be sure that wax does not make any area in the bathroom slippery.

Shelf Lining—Use sheet linoleum (you can buy it in smaller pieces at places like K-Mart) to line your shelves. If you have a kitchen cabinet that has an open space above the top cabinet, be sure to cover this or it will get REALLY dirty and greasy.

Dirty Tub—Clean it right after using, before body oil has a chance to harden. You can even start the cleaning while you are in the tub. Don't use slippery cleanser while you are still in the tub, though. Don't use any harsh cleanser on any tub made before 1964. It will remove the finish. Believe me, I speak from experience.

Vacuum Easier—Use an upright vacuum like Regina, Hoover, or Eureka. The uprights are so much easier to put away and get out that you will be inclined to vacuum more often because it's not "too much trouble" to get this kind of vacuum out for a little job. If you have an upstairs, keep one of the lightweight upright vacuums that can be hung from the wall in an upstairs closet on the second floor for easy access.

Books on Housekeeping

Aslett, Don. *Is There Life After Housework?* Cincinnati, Ohio: Writers Digest Books, 1981.

An absolute must as a "how to" book on cleaning. Not to be used until you have become organized enough to get around to these jobs he tells us how to do so quickly and so well.

Brace, Pam, and Jones, Peggy. *Sidetracked Home Executives, From Pigpen to Paradise.* Vancouver: Binford and Mort, 1979 (188 pages).

This is a funny, helpful approach that works for people who have a housekeeping problem. Furthermore, the writers speak from experience.

Conran, Shirley. *Superwoman, For Every Woman Who Hates Housework.* New York: Crown Publishers, Inc., 1978 (270 pages).

This is a big, expensive book which ends up sounding as if it was written for women who *love* housework. It has some helpful items, however, and covers many topics.

Editors of Consumer Guide. *The Fastest, Cheapest, Best Way to Clean Everything.* New York: Fireside, Simon & Schuster, 1982.

If I could buy only three books on housekeeping, this would be one of them. It names brands and tells how to use them. By the way, the other two books I'd buy would be *The Messies Manual* and *Is There Life After Housework?*

McBride, Pat. *How to Get Your Act Together When Nobody Gave You the Script.* Nashville: Thomas Nelson Publishers, 1982 (167 pages).

A clearly written book dealing with time management as it applies to the home. A good supplement to reading on this subject.

McCullough, Bonnie Runyan. *Bonnie's Household Organizer.* New York: St. Martin's Press, 1980 (181 pages).

This work is especially valuable because it has four chapters on training children and it is strong in the areas of creating storage space and organizing cupboards.

McCullough, Bonnie Runyan, and Monson, Susan Walker. *401 Ways to Get Your Kids to Work at Home.* New York: St. Martin's Press, 1981 (245 pages).

This book touches on and explains further many of the ideas mentioned in *The Messies Manual.* It's good.

Pinkham, Mary Ellen. *Mary Ellen's Best of Helpful Hints.* New York: Warner Books, Inc., 1980 (125 pages).

Lots of hints about lots of things, helpfully indexed. There will be many ideas you can use.

Winston, Stephanie. *Getting Organized.* New York: Warner Books, Inc., 1978.

One of the best books I have found on the subject, it is widely known and frequently mentioned in the paper. A strong and valuable section is the one called *Time and Paperwork* since it deals with how to handle the various paper items that come into the house and group themselves in little piles.

MORE HELP FROM
MESSIES ANONYMOUS

If you would like a free Messies Anonymous sample newsletter with information about obtaining the complete Messies Anonymous Flipper Kit and other helps available from Messies Anonymous, write to:

MESSIES ANONYMOUS™
5025 S.W. 114 Avenue
Miami, Florida 33165